110664834

FRANCIS CLINTON

A Buffalo Soldier, and American Hero

BY

ARCHIETTA BURCH JAMES

Copyright © 2021 Archietta Burch James

All rights reserved.

Table Of Contents

Dedication

THIS BOOK IS DEDICATED TO FRANCIS CLINTON AND ALL HIS
DESCENDANTS

THIS BOOK IS DEDICATED TO ALL BUFFALO SOLDIERS AND
THEIR DESCENDANTS

THIS BOOK IS ALSO DEDICATED TO ALL EDUCATORS AND
STUDENTS THAT THIRST FOR UNDISCOVERED KNOWLEDGE

Acknowledgments

There is no way possible to properly thank everyone who helped make this book project successful. I am truly grateful for this journey into the life of Francis Clinton, my great grandfather, the heroic Buffalo Soldier. I am grateful to be one of Francis' descendants. I am very thankful to the Creator for the vision.

I would like to thank my immediate family members, my husband Clarence James Jr., my son John Aaron James, my daughter Iman L. James and my granddaughter Jaylah James for all their support and encouragement while I burned mid-night oil and many long hours toiling to complete this book. I would like to thank all my family members for the knowledge they shared, and the many stories told and passed down from generation to generation about my great grandfather Francis Clinton: Clara Clinton Jackson Spencer (his daughter and my grandmother), Cleo Jackson Burch (his granddaughter and my mother), Uncle Eugene and Aunt Idella Jackson, Carl Jackson that called on his great sprit while he fought in the military. Sharon Love (my sister) and John James (my son) for writing term papers on him in high school and college. Archie Jr. T. Burch, my brother, for inspiring me to write the Francis Clinton Story. Thanks to Archie Jr. III, my nephew, for gathering information on Francis' life at several military bases during his tour of duty. Thanks to my siblings for their support, Brenda Burch Smith, Vernal Williams, Ruby Oliver, Samuel and Elton Burch. Thanks to all my family members involved in the many road trips to the various forts/garrisons and museums to take a walk in Francis Clinton's boots. My traveling crew or entourage was packed and ready to go at the drop of a hat. Traveling crew involved: Alvin Love, Sharon Love, Vernal Williams, John James, Jaylah James, Iman James, Leanna Lundy James, and Clarence James. Thanks to Equalla Clinton (my cousin and her great grandfather for researching the archives and gathering family documents and records). Thanks to Stephanie Tania Smith, niece, for writing the Francis Clinton poem. Thanks to Joyce Shelton Williams for helping me get started and continued to inspire me to write the "Francis Clinton Story." Thanks to Julie Jackson for assisting as my reading critic. Also, I would like to thank: Tairia Burch Kelso, niece, for the book cover photograph, Kaleb Woolfolk, nephew, for helping with the book cover graphic design, Shundrika Love, niece, and my makeup artist, and Joe Luna, my photographer.

Thanks, Arnishia and Mickey Jr. Oliver, for supporting the Francis Clinton Story by using his story in school projects with Mee Mee and Skylar. Thanks to the tour guides for their assistance, guidance, and knowledge.

Sorry in advance if I forgot to thank anyone that helped with this book project. This book has been forthcoming for a long time. It started to develop years ago when I was a child and heard many stories about great grandfather Clinton before I read anything about the Buffalo Soldiers. It has been extremely hard work writing this book. Although writing this book has been a long and grueling process, it was a wonderful and rewarding experience. This book has enlightened us about the hidden history of Black heroes like the Buffalo Soldiers that has never been told.

Introduction

This book is about my great grandfather Francis Clinton that was one of the original Buffalo Soldiers. The Francis Clinton story exists today only because my family kept his legacy alive by telling and retelling his story to the different generations through word of mouth. Stories about him as a famous Buffalo Soldier were told and passed down from generation to generation by family members. I am forever grateful that Gramma Clara and my mother Cleo shared his story among our family. Otherwise, we would not have known anything about him. Francis Clinton played a very important role in the American military and the history of America and was never given credit for his contributions nor mentioned in any history books. Through a tremendous amount of research and miles and miles of traveling, I was able to gather information on the life of Francis Clinton to write this book. Francis served in the US Navy and with the United States 10th Cavalry, Company E, as one of the original famous Buffalo Soldiers. The heroic Buffalo Soldiers contributed to American History by shaping the Western Frontier.

Francis Clinton Unforgotten Buffalo Soldier

The Buffalo Soldiers are a part of history that's unspoken

A big part of History with a very small token.

The things they did to help America get built

The lives that were given and the blood that was spilled.

The Buffalo Soldiers and the 10th Cavalry, Company E

Helped to build America, this Country.

Without their bravery, valor, and sacrifice

America may not have become our homely paradise.

My Great Great Grandfather Francis Clinton

Was among those Buffalo Soldiers, America forgot to mention.

Considered by his Commander Benjamin Grierson

Francis was one of the best cavalrymen he ever had.

To not mention these famous Buffalo Soldiers is just so sad!

- Stephanie Tania Smith

Chapter 1: Naval Years (1865– 1867)

When I was young, my Gramma Clara Clinton Jackson Spencer would tell me and my siblings exhilarating stories about Francis Clinton, our great grandfather. One story that I remember specifically was about him fighting a battle in the Indian war on the Washita River. During the battle, he fell off his horse and ruptured his side. He started bleeding, but instead of giving up, he jumped back on his horse and continued fighting. Sometimes Gramma Clara's stories were a bit far-fetched, like he single-handedly fought mountain lions. Other times he would carry heavy sacks of feed on his bare shoulders to feed the livestock on their farm. As I grew older, the stories became more somber and less fanciful. I realized that Francis Clinton beat insurmountable odds in the face of racism and brutality. He chose to live a life on his own terms and conditions. He served in the United States Navy and in the 10th Cavalry, Company E, as one of America's famous Buffalo Soldiers. Though, despite his extraordinary accomplishments, he was never recognized and remembered in American history. My great grandfather lived an extraordinary life of courage and valor. I know that his life as a Buffalo Soldier was incredibly amazing. I made a vow to myself that I would seek out information about his life and narrate his amazing story to the world by retracing his journey whenever the opportunity presented itself.

After I retired from teaching in 2016, I started to earnestly research and gather knowledge about his life and the legendary Buffalo Soldiers. As a literary teacher, I felt obligated and compelled to share his story with the world. Sometimes during my reading classes, I would share stories with my students about my great grandfather's heroic service as a famous Buffalo Soldier. Many of my students would often ask me why the schools don't teach more about the Buffalo Soldiers and their contributions to America. I do not have an answer to why the school systems do not include the Buffalo Soldiers and their contributions to America in their curriculum. So, I knew I had a duty and commitment as an educator to write this book. Even though my mother, Cleo Vearneta Jackson Burch, and her mother, Gramma Clara, had shared many stories about him with the family, I needed to personally research his life. I brainstormed about how to write Francis' life story, but I met a dead end every time until God appeared to me in a dream. My dream was to travel and visit the most prominent garrisons and bases where Francis served and start with the last garrison, which was Fort Concho in San Angelo, Texas, and end with his first Naval base, which was the Historic Ships in Baltimore, Maryland. Yes, Francis started his military career in the US Navy as a porter on the CSS/USS Albemarle and the USS Constellation.

From the beginning of American history, Black men participated in the nautical strengthening of the new republic's endeavors. They worked on mercantile and warships, contributing to commerce and defending American interests. On the Civil War threshold, African Americans recognized that they could finally achieve their most significant objectives in the struggle for independence, liberty, and equality. Both free and enslaved African Americans were looking towards a future where they could live life as a free citizen. Ordinary Americans were becoming aware of the evil of slavery and had come to realize that slavery was an ungodly and barbaric system fit for no one. The war provided African American men opportunities for advancement. In some instances, it came in the form of freedom from slavery, and in others, financial reparations or property. They played an essential part, first in creating a free country and then in defending the freedom of that country. Ironically, their own freedom was repeatedly denied and revoked.

Francis Clinton was born in 1842 in Baltimore, Maryland. Not much is known about his early years, but it comes as no surprise that he was familiar with ships and sea lanes from a young age. At that time, the largest number of African American men to enlist in the Navy were from Maryland. With its many tributaries and Baltimore's port, Chesapeake Bay's maritime culture made Marylander's ideal for working in all aspects of maritime undertakings.

Around 1863 – 1865, Francis Clinton enlisted in the Union Navy in New Bern, North Carolina. The Union held areas in North Carolina, Plymouth, Washington,

Beaufort, Morehead City, Roanoke Island, and New Bern, which attracted large numbers of contrabands. The Union forces employed many of the refugees as laborers, teamsters, servants, laundresses, or skilled craftsmen, as well as scouts, spies, soldiers, or sailors. More than 5000 African American men joined the Union army during that period.

The United States military used the term contraband during the Civil War to define the status of escaped slaves or other African American military men allied with Union forces. In 1861, the Union military decided that escaped sailors who wished to side with the Union would no longer be returned to their slave owners and were categorized as the "contraband of war" or "spoils of war." The Union forces used many of the escapees as labor and eventually started to pay them a standard wage. Thousands of former slaves encamped near the Union forces, and the military helped educate and support the adults and children of the refugees. After the Emancipation Proclamation in 1863, scores of African American men from the refugee camps flocked to enlist with the United States Colored Troop (USCT). By the end of the war, there were more than a hundred contraband camps in the South, including the self-sufficient settlement of Freedmen's Colony of Roanoke Island.

Francis, my great grandfather, enlisted in the Navy and served on the CSS/USS Albemarle and the USS Constellation for two years. This was during the times when the Civil War was ravaging the whole country. According to his pension application, he worked as a Porter (cleaner) aboard the ship. Black men were blocked from serving in the United States Army, and the army did not remedy this condition until 1862. However, African American sailors were allowed to enlist in the Continental Navy after the War of 1812, although their numbers were limited to 5% of all Navy enlistments. Angry at their inability to join the Union Army and fight for their freedom, Black men rushed to enlist in the Union Navy in the early days of the Civil War. The Constellation's muster roll shows that 15 African Americans served aboard her during the war period.

Learning about the history of the CSS/USS Albemarle and the USS Constellation made me feel so proud that my great grandfather served aboard these historic ships. Both ships were an essential part of his story and American history. The mere fact that Francis did whatever it took to survive during those horrific times made me realize how courageous he actually was. His survival skills were astonishing. He served aboard a ship that was once a part of the slave trade and a vessel that was a steam-powered gunboat ram. He made decisions to do things that were necessary to survive. I exist today because of his profound decision-making skills, fortitude, persistence, courage, and perseverance.

The CSS/USS Albemarle was a steam-powered ironclad gunboat ram of the Confederate Navy (and later the second Albemarle of the United States Navy), named for a town and a sound in North Carolina. This vessel was designed to (wrest) control of North Carolina's sounds from the Federal forces that had dominated the region since 1862. Construction of the ironclad began in a cornfield at Edwards's Ferry on the Roanoke River in January 1863. The Albemarle was built to be a ram, this being her foremost weapon. Her underlying structure consisted of oak timbers covered over in iron plates. The iron ram protruded from her bow and was shaped like the head of an ax. In a nutshell, she was designed to smash through the sides of wooden ships. It had destructive powers that could sink an enemy vessel quickly.

After the war, the Union gunboat USS Ceres towed the Albemarle to Norfolk, Va. April 1865. She was repaired in August 1865, but the Navy Department decided to sell her at auction for scrap in October of 1867. Her only parts of having survived the war were a cannon and her smokestack, the latter on display today at the Albemarle Museum in Elizabeth City, North Carolina. And she left behind a legacy that is still talked about in high notes in the history books.

The USS Constellation was constructed in 1854 as a sloop-of-war. The Constellation is the last sail-only warship designed and built by the U.S. Navy. She was built in the Gosport Navy Yard at Portsmouth and was launched on August 26, 1854. The USS Constellation is a large warship that was commissioned in 1855. The 22-gun sloop was active for 100 years and served in several military conflicts. My great grandfather Francis served on the USS Constellation. This ship was heavily involved in the Slave Trade Patrol.

When my great grandfather Francis served in the Navy, Gideon Welles was Secretary of the United States Navy, cabinet member for the presidencies of Abraham Lincoln and Andrew Johnson.   Welles served as secretary from 1861 to 1869. He developed the Navy into a force that could successfully execute blockades of Southern ports, which was a critical factor in the North's Civil War victory. He was also instrumental in constructing the ironclad USS Monitor and the establishment of the Navy's Medal of Honor. President Lincoln ordered Welles to pursue a naval strangulation blockade of the South aggressively. It was part of Lincoln's key strategy. Welles's agents brought any suitable vessel which could be filled with a gun, and he and his staff recruited admirals, officers, and crews to man this Navy in its process of creation. Within years, they created a powerful Navy of the North, having some of the bravest men onboard.

Welles's administration of the Navy was successful. He adopted modern methods of coastal warfare and innovation vessels. Ironclad steam-powered vessels supported by shallow draft monitors closed port after port and cleared rivers in the South, fulfilling President Lincoln's orders. The Navy had grown from 45 or so service-worthy vessels to 671 and 7,600 sailors in just four years, making it a first-class power. President Lincoln referred to Welles as "Neptune" after the ancient God said to rule the sea.

During these times, African American recruits, along with my great grandfather, had to endure covert discriminatory obstacles that were rooted in systemic racism. However, I would like to mention here that discrimination and segregation were minimal in the Union Navy. African American sailors lived and ate with their white counterparts and sometimes held rank over white shipmen. Nevertheless, prejudice and hate seeped through from civilian life. Some commanding officers held an ingrained bias against African American shipmen and used underhanded tactics at every opportunity. Although the Union Navy had not codified a formal method of racial separation, segregation stemmed from the rules related to African American sailors' recruiting and rating. The guidelines and rules issued by Sec. Welles reaffirmed existing prejudices that African American's were by nature inferior and submissive by relegating African American sailors to serve in unskilled and menial jobs. At the time of enlistment, recruiters gave a rating to the enlistee based on their naval experience. Those with no prior experience were given the ratings of boys or landsmen, and those with experience were given a rating as ordinary seamen and above. Eighty-two percent of African American sailors were rated as boys and landsmen, even with previous know-how and experience. Even though the sailors were promised $10 per month, the recruits only earned $1 or $2 per month. The remainder was docked from their pay and spent on their room and board and towards their families' upkeep.

African American shipmen constituted a sizeable percentage in a very dangerous, exploited, and low-paid occupation. Several accounts relate to the appalling working conditions of African American sailors, unduly strenuous work, unwarranted fees for food and lodging, ruthless and cruel officers, and innumerable other indignities. The most severe danger was if the Confederate Navy captured an African American sailor, the prisoners were never heard from again in many cases. When the Civil War ended in 1865, African American shipmen had served on almost 700 Navy vessels. African Americans accounted for more than 10 percent of the Navy's enlistment strength. Eight of them even earned the Medal of Honor for valor in combat. Despite all of this, many of their contributions have been disregarded and unrecognized by Historians.

However, the United States Navy overlooked the actual number of African American shipmen who had served during the Civil War. With the help of the Naval Historical Center, Howard University, National Park Service, and recently discovered documentation, the number of enlisted African Americans were revised to 18,000, almost double the initial count. On November 17, 2000, a ceremony was held at the Navy Memorial in Washington, D.C., and 8000 forgotten African American sailors – including a dozen women – were added to its roll of honored Civil War veterans.

The USS Constellation is preserved as a National Historic Landmark in Baltimore, Maryland. The USS Constellation, which is currently docked at pier one along the Inner Harbor, was first launched in 1854 and has had a tenuous history throughout its active life. The last all-sail ship in the U.S. Navy, the Constellation, once played a role in disrupting the slave trade and has seen duty in both world wars. Today, visitors can climb aboard and tour the decks and play the part of a 19th-century sailor.

In 2018, I contacted the Historic Ships of Baltimore Museum and registered as a descendent of Francis Clinton, a Civil War veteran. I started receiving their Deck Log Newsletters to get regular updates about events happening on the ship. In July, they have the 4th of July Independence Deck Celebration, which I thought would be an awesome event for my family to attend. I made plans for my family to visit the ship and participate in the Fourth of July Celebration. My plans were for the family, Francis Clinton's descendants, to visit and tour the USS Constellation on July 4, 2020. I wanted the family to see and experience the celebratory event honoring our relative that served aboard this historic ship. All my plans were canceled because of the global coronavirus pandemic. Due to the countrywide lockdown, the only viable option was for me to take a virtual tour of the USS Constellation.

During my simulated virtual tour, I imagined the wind on my face as the USS Constellation sailed across the sea. I could hear the wooden clap of my shoes as I walked on her deck. The same deck that my great grandfather might have polished with pride. I imagined the echoes of his footsteps as he walked towards the berth or stargazed with his shipmates. I imagined him quietly observing all his descendants gathered for the 4th of July Independence Deck Party, the ship reverberating with the happy voices of so many of his progeny and his spirit at peace with all he had helped create. What a proud image!

Visualizing this moment and knowing what Francis had accomplished makes me realize that this is only the beginning of his fantastic story. My desire to write this book about Francis Clinton's life is to reveal the many contributions he made in the United States military as a pioneer blazing the way for others to follow. He served in the Navy and helped open doors for African American sailors. After serving in the Navy, he served 16 years in the United States Cavalry as one of our famous original Buffalo Soldiers. Let us never forget or overlook the outstanding contributions that he made for this country. So, onward and forward to his life as a famous Buffalo Soldier! Fort Leavenworth in Kansas.

"WHAT I DO ABOUT SLAVERY…I DO…IF IT HELPS TO SAVE THE UNION."

- Abraham Lincoln

CSS Albemarle

*Francis Clinton served on of the USS Constellation and the Albemarle around about the
end of the Civil War.*

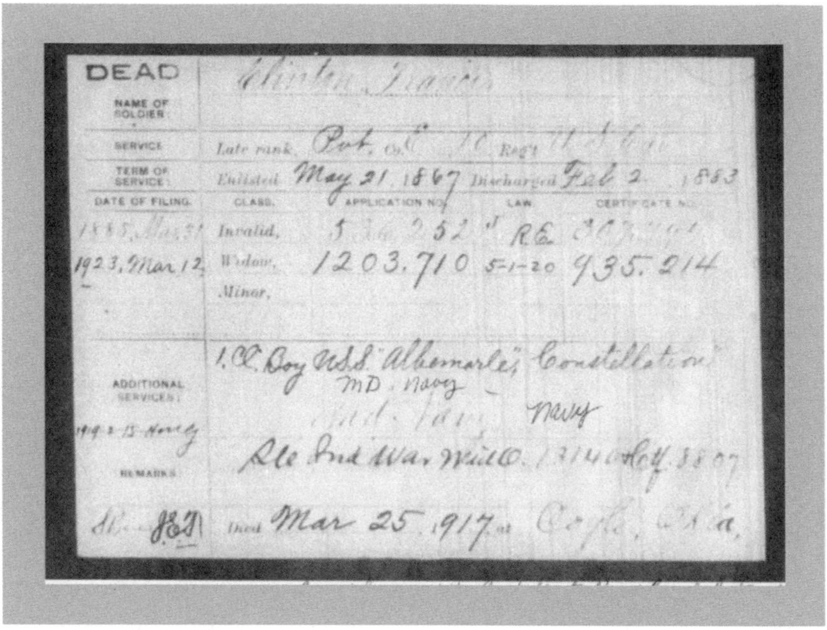
DEAD

NAME OF SOLDIER:

SERVICE: Late rank, Pvt. Co. E 10 Reg't

TERM OF SERVICE: Enlisted May 21, 1867 Discharged Feb 2, 1883

DATE OF FILING.	CLASS.	APPLICATION NO.	LAW.	CERTIFICATE NO.
1885, Mar 31	Invalid,	[illegible]		[illegible]
1923, Mar 12	Widow,	1203.710	5-1-20	935.214
	Minor,			

ADDITIONAL SERVICES: 1 Cl. Boy U.S.S. "Albemarle", "Constellation" MD. Navy

Navy

REMARKS:

Died Mar 25, 1917 at [illegible]

Death Certificate of Buffalo Soldier

Chapter 2: Fort Leavenworth (1867)

According to my mother, Verneta Cleo Jackson Burch, and her mother, Gramma Clara, my great grandfather, Francis Clinton, was proud that he served in the US Navy. He had this appetite of fighting for his nation's peace, stability, and for a more significant cause i.e., the freedom for the African American community. His tales showcased his exhilarating experiences on the war front, fighting on the regions' vast seas. His success was not just a victory for the US Navy but also for the entire African American community that hoped to be an essential part of the nation's pride.

Francis often told Gramma Clara that he always wanted to spend his life protecting his family, serving, and fighting for his country. When he was a young boy, he had a yearning to enlist in the United States Army. He wanted to be at the front end of the battles, fighting the enemies of the nation and be among the heroes of the nation. As an African American, he had a long way to go in order to convert his dream into a reality. There was a prominent issue of discrimination and systematic racism that stood in between him and his dreams. The prehistoric segregation laws of the United States did not just disappear overnight. Even though slavery was abolished, there was still a long way to go for the proper recognition and appreciation of the African American Community. One such prehistoric law prevented people of color from being enlisted in the US Army. Yes, despite the sheer hard work and countless contributions during the Civil War by the African American men and women as patriots in the Union Army and US Navy, the laws still prohibited their enlisting in the United States Army.

It took Congress about a year to finally understand the importance of a massive army in maintaining peace across the country. Finally, they realized that it wasn't possible without getting the African American community on board. During my research, I found some really astonishing facts about how Congress eventually decided that African Americans could participate in the United States Army. According to the figures, there was a point after the civil war when the United States Army decreased to just 16000, which was evidently not enough for the protection of the country's peacemaking and stability following the civil war. Especially with the growing unrest in the southern and westerns parts of the country. Eventually, there were hot debates across Congress; many expressed in favor of integration while others, although less, still advocated for segregation. Looking back to this moment, it's beyond me how people would act and discriminate based on a persons' skin color. However, I am not so surprised considering how people still, to this date, hold such disgusting, discriminatory, and exclusionary thinking in their minds. Nevertheless, through my research, I found out that the discussions had gotten hotter in Congress, and despite the majority in favor of complete integration of people of different races, they had to go with the voice of the minority that held racial views. Basically, the country had just gone through a civil war phase, and it was too early for Congress to take such radical steps. Politicians, army officials, officers, basically white people in principal offices analyzed and scrutinized African Americans' participation in the Civil War. They analyzed their every move, every error, their achievements, and their failures, and so on, but of course, they could not hold anything against them. They knew that the success and active participation of the African Americans in the Civil War meant that each and every single person of the African American community was worthy of being a part of the United States Army. They realized that each one of them fought with valor, courage, strength and gave away everything they had to keep the United States flag waving high.

Finally, after many debates and discussions, Congress passed the legislation that would sit well with both the supporters and the opposition. The act known as the Army Reorganization Act was passed in 1866. The Regular Army ranks were doubled, and six regiments were set up, which were purely meant to enlist African American soldiers. These regulated regiments were the 9th and 10th Cavalry and the 38th, 39th, 40th, and 41st Infantry. My great grandfather, Francis Clinton, enlisted in the 10th Cavalry, Company E of the United States Army. Researching the facts about my grandfather's life, makes me feel so elated knowing that he was part of this US Army's historical moment, but yet, at the same time, I feel disappointed that Francis and many other African American heroes have not been recognized in American History. First, he served the Union by joining the US Navy during the Civil War and later became one of the first African American soldiers to enlist in the United States Army officially. He joined the 10th Cavalry, Troop E, of the United States Army, which later became known as the famous Buffalo Soldiers. My great grandfather's journey into being a part of such a tremendous revolutionary regiment began with the formation of the Buffalo Soldiers.

The 10th Cavalry was formed in September 1866 at Fort Leavenworth, Kansas, and became one of the most iconic regiments in the history of the United States of America. The 10th Cavalry has many outstanding achievements to its name, especially in advancing a modern civilization in America's last continental frontier, the West. They were also responsible for guarding the construction workers that were setting up the rail tracks, protecting towns, building army forts, and providing security to the western posts from the raiders and marauders. Before I unfold the story of an unsung American hero, Francis Clinton, I would like to familiarize my readers with the history of the Buffalo Soldiers.

The 10th Cavalry was formed during the period when the regiments were being set. African Americans were being scrutinized, trained, and recruited in the US Army. Benjamin Grierson was appointed as the first commander of the 10th Cavalry. Grierson is mentioned in US history as one of the greatest war heroes, and I am glad to know that Francis was under his command and guidance. Grierson was a strong supporter of the integration of armies. He even fought alongside African Americans during the Civil War and led them to victory on many skirmishes. After the war, he openly and eagerly advocated for health, education, rights, and better living conditions for the newly freed African American men and women. Moreover, Grierson was also one of the white officers who testified for the integration of the armies in front of Congress during the debates. There could not have been a much better leader to train and command the 10th Cavalry Regiment.

Grierson knew that he needed some loyal and trustworthy recruits to command at Fort Leavenworth. Therefore, before taking command, he appointed and recruited officers at St. Louis. He knew he had troubling times ahead of him with the regiment's growth and development. He was appointed the responsibility to command the first official fighting African American Regiment. He also knew that there were many in the ranks of the Army that were not happy with this integration and that they would make things difficult for him. He wasn't wrong as Colonel William Hoffman, the Third Infantry Regimental Commander and the post commander at Fort Leavenworth, became a huge obstacle for Grierson and the regiment because of his racial bias and prehistoric exclusionary ways.

Hoffman first showed his racial prejudice back during the Civil War when he refused to appoint any African American to his company. He was the Commissary General of Prisoners back then. The first huge problem that came in the way of the 10th Cavalry at the hands of Hoffman was that he provided the African American soldiers with an unsuitable terrain to train in a swampy area in the post's lower grounds. The place was very damp, moist, humid, and difficult to set up camp and train the incoming recruits. However, Grierson decided to abide by it initially. However, Hoffman's discrimination and racism didn't stop here. He continued to bully Grierson and his supporting officers during their whole service time at Fort Leavenworth.

Can you imagine how difficult it must have been for them? I know that it wasn't easy for the Buffalo Soldiers to reside in such a muddy, swampy, and low area of the Fort. Who likes sloshing in mud when it rains? They had to sleep on the moist, swampy grounds away from the white barracks as per Hoffman's orders. It's hard to imagine how difficult it must have been for the Regiment to live in those intolerable conditions. According to what I know about Francis is that he was determined to withstand all stones thrown at him, even racial prejudice, because of his strong will to serve his country and its people. He wanted to represent every single African American who struggled and dreamed of being a part of the country's pride. That showcases the love and respect he had for his country.

As per my research, during the recruitment process at the Fort, Grierson experienced more trouble. He didn't like the way the set appointment and commission processes were being handled. According to Grierson, the set rules put a hurdle in the hiring process of his regiment. He felt it limited his opportunities and ability to recruit officers for his regiment. His first duty was to appoint the right officers for the 10th. He had to hire people who wouldn't let their prejudice come in their way and would work in the best interests of the 10th. After successfully appointing a force, he sent out Lieutenants all across the States, such as Ohio, for enlisting the soldiers. Grierson worked tirelessly for the 10th Cavalry. On his trips across the country, he would try to convince as many veterans as he could to commission for the 10th. He tried to make sure that the camp received adequate supplies, equipment, and resources so that they could start preparing for the training as soon as the enlisted soldiers arrived. By 1867, Grierson was successfully able to establish and train eight companies at Fort Leavenworth. He created the other four at their next station, Fort Riley. My great grandfather joined the 10th Cavalry on January 15, 1867.

Research shows that Grierson was a tough commander, and he expected a lot from his recruits. He also had high standards and didn't enlist just anyone and everyone. I feel a special pride knowing Francis was able to meet Grierson's standards, fulfill his checklist, and successfully enlist in the 10th Cavalry. Recruits began training as soon as they reached the site, serving the country, and that too under Grierson wasn't easy. I can imagine Francis fulfilling all his duties, tasks, and training with full vigor. I can see him falling but not giving up, and I can see him rising, pushing forward, facing each task head-on and with bravery. I can see him fighting along with his team, keeping everyone together while leading from the front. According to Gramma Clara, Private Clinton spoke about how his squad would look up to him and how his cavalry brothers sought inspiration from him. She told us how Francis didn't just carry himself towards each success, but he carried every one of his companions and peers with him. The tasks were exhausting, challenging, and a true test for these recruits. Daily activities included a total of three assemblies, drills, fatigue details, special assignments, and guard duty. Looking at Fort Leavenworth virtually, I can imagine my great grandfather and his company all assembled, standing with pride in the morning sun and marching with their chests out. I can even imagine Francis with his head up high and his hand on the US emblem as the band played the Reveille. A wonderfully warm-hearted feeling consumes me when I think about this amazing scenario. I can just imagine him in his uniform standing tall, bursting with pride to know that he's a member of this incredible unit of cavalrymen.

An essential part of the unit's training involved guard duty. Guard duty was the most crucial task at Fort Leavenworth, and Grierson would make sure that every soldier was appointed to guard duty. Gramma would tell us, and so does my research, that Francis really enjoyed guard duty. Whenever he was assigned the task, he felt excited as adrenaline rushed through his body. He also felt proud that he could be trusted with such an essential task of guarding and defending their base. Grierson would personally inspect and evaluate each recruit and their duties. I remember learning that Grierson would personally come up to each recruit and question them on their responsibilities. I can feel the second-hand anxiety just thinking about Francis being put on the spot and evaluated. Imagine standing in the presence of a war hero and being subjected to rapid questions about your duties and tasks. I would totally flinch or faint under pressure. However, I'm sure Francis faced this courageously and confidently. I can see Grierson pat his back whenever Private Clinton proved himself to be a worthy member and soldier of the 10th Cavalry.

Grierson would hold drills to prevent soldier boredom, just to keep them active, alert, and on their feet. It also prevented them from loafing around and wasting time. These drills were an excellent way of building team spirit and learning what it truly means to be a soldier. However, things were never smooth at the Fort; the horses and resources sent their way were usually substandard, which made training a taxing and challenging task. Grierson's attention was diverted from the soldiers to administrative and management issues. Soldiers started getting stressed out about the unbearable living conditions. Even though Grierson was proving to be a skillful leader, he could see that the recruits were losing their morale. Most came to the Fort all exhilarated and pumped up about being in the US Cavalry but would soon start losing their excitement. Grierson knew that it was all because of post-Commander Hoffman's monstrous attitude and racial prejudice as he would not let go of a single chance to pull down the morale of the African American recruits. He was unprofessional and abusive to the soldiers. He would intervene in Grierson's business, and despite trying to come to an agreement, Hoffman continued to become an obstacle for Grierson and his troops. Grierson was later forced to write to the higher ranks and requested that they allow him to make his own decisions and bypass Hoffman because he continued to intervene and sabotage Grierson. Hoffman was enraged at Grierson's defiance and his letter to the superiors. Growing tension infuriated Hoffman even more, and he tried to get Grierson court-martialed, but thankfully that didn't happen.

Hoffman's growing resentment for the 10th Cavalry and how he continuously tried to sabotage or delay any of the regimental achievements were unbearable. Grierson was left with no other choice but to request a transfer with his regiment. He made the arrangements for the 10th Cavalry and all the companies to be transferred to Fort Riley not too far from Leavenworth, where he could continue the recruitment process and train the soldiers to their full potential. Personally, I cannot even imagine how awful and disappointing it must've felt for the kind of treatment Grierson and his company received while they were stationed at Fort Leavenworth. Even after the abolishment of slavery, some white people, such as Hoffman, continued to see people of color as the 'inferior' and didn't want to see them rise and succeed. I am sure it took a lot of patience for Francis to endure the daily struggles he faced because of systemic racism. That probably required a lot more strength, patience, and tolerance just to bear the racial prejudice they were all experiencing collectively. I am grateful they had a leader like Grierson. Gramma shared with us how Francis would never stop singing praises about Grierson, how if it was not for him, all the Cavalry would have lost hope. Maybe they would have succumbed to Hoffman's tyranny and racism. Perhaps even worse, they could have taken some wrong steps that could have led to another all-out battle. Nevertheless, I am glad that they moved from Fort Leavenworth and Hoffman's command. This particular decision by Grierson proved to be beneficial for the regiment as well as all the African American troops.

Fort Leavenworth continues to stay active today as a military base under the US Army. The Buffalo Soldiers' legacy continued despite Hoffman and others who tried to oppose them and erase their achievements.

My plans are to visit Fort Leavenworth in the near future and see the swampy grounds where Private Clinton and his regiment trained. I intend to tour the fort, breathe the air, and walk in the space where my great grandfather was recruited. To be able to walk through the swamp and experience what it was like for the 10th Cavalry would be my way of reliving his memory. I am sure I would be able to sense great grandfather Francis' presence at the fort when I go for the visit. There's a saying about great people, they leave their mark and presence at every place they go. Although, I hear the swamp area is now a nice jogging track. I can imagine Francis and I jogging on the track, visiting about what life was like for him and his regiment back in the cavalry formation days. I wish Francis and his cavalry brothers could see the beautiful track today!

Today, this same spot where my great grandfather used to slumber with his regiment has become a historical site. There now stands a 16-foot bronze statue of a Black cavalryman pulling back his horse's reins. Eddie Dixon, a Black sculptor, created the statue. It took him a total of two and a half years to finish this historic statue. Looking at the statue virtually, my eyes glow with satisfaction, content, pride, and joy, knowing that this statue is a symbolic figure of my great grandfather. I am glad to see that we have come a long way from the times when African Americans had zero rights in the United States to the current era, where people have started recognizing the efforts of African Americans. I know we have made some strides, even though we still have a long way to go. I am proud and joyous to know that in my body runs the blood of a National Hero, Francis Clinton, who helped make all of this possible for us. His contributions are the reason why we are here today.

This is just the beginning of his fascinating and triumphant life. My quest of unveiling the story of Francis takes us to our next destination where he moved on with his regiment and Grierson, Fort Riley!

"Let the Black man get an eagle on his button, and there is no power on earth which can deny that he has earned the right to citizenship in the United States."

-Frederick Douglas

Francis Clinton 1842-1917

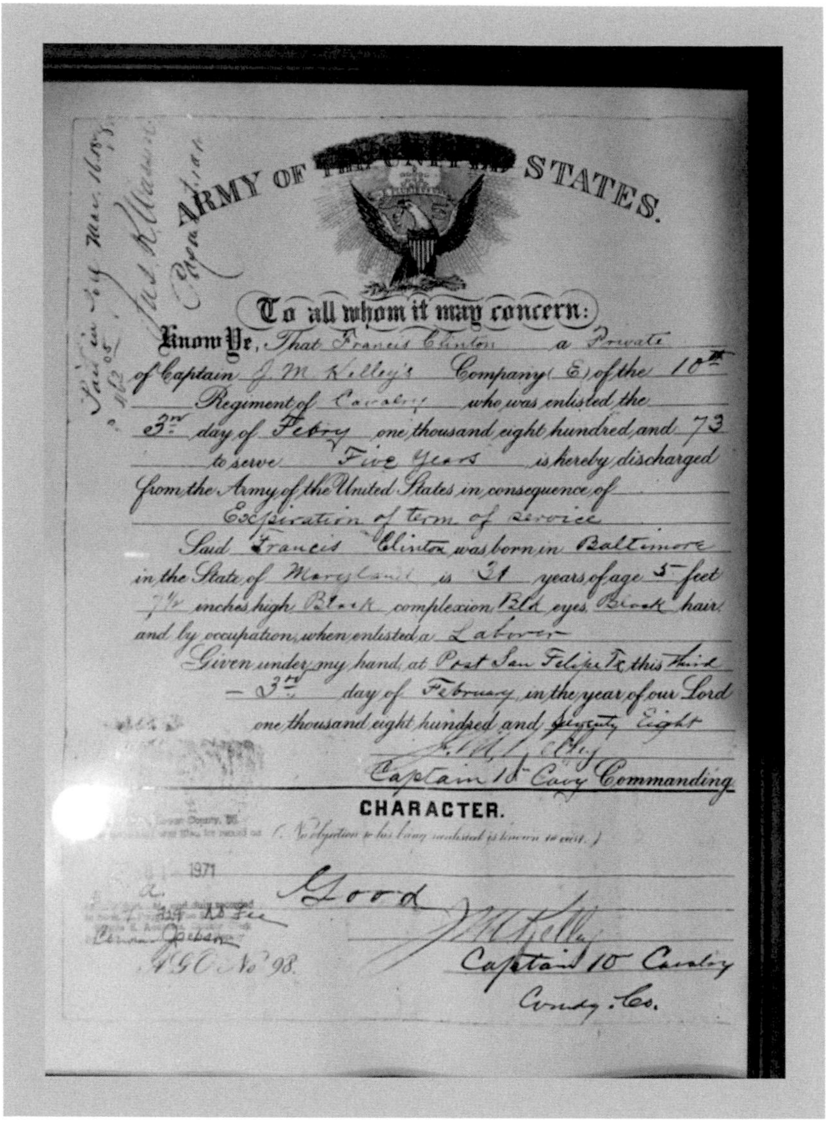

ARMY OF [illegible] STATES.

To all whom it may concern:

Know Ye, That Francis Clinton a Private of Captain J. M. Kelley's Company (E) of the 10th Regiment of Cavalry who was enlisted the 3rd day of Febry one thousand eight hundred and 73 to serve Five Years is hereby discharged from the Army of the United States in consequence of Expiration of term of service

Said Francis Clinton was born in Baltimore in the State of Maryland is 31 years of age 5 feet 7¼ inches high Black complexion Blk eyes Black hair and by occupation, when enlisted a Laborer

Given under my hand at Post San Felipe Tx this third – 3rd day of February in the year of our Lord one thousand eight hundred and Seventy Eight

J. M. Kelley
Captain 10th Cavy Commanding

CHARACTER.

(No objection to his being reenlisted is known to exist.)

Good

J. M. Kelley
Captain 10 Cavalry
Comdg. Co.

AGO No 98.

Francis Clinton Service Letter

Col. Benjamin H. Grierson organized the Tenth United Stated Cavalry

Statue of Buffalo Soldier in Fort Leavenworth - Sculpted by Eddie Dixon

Chapter 3: Fort Riley (1867–1868)

Hoffman's hostile behavior towards the 10th Cavalry and especially the African American troops became unbearable for Grierson's regiment to succeed. Grierson could feel the increasing restlessness and panic in his regiment, and the only viable option for him was to move his unit out of Fort Leavenworth. Therefore, the feasible option at that time was Fort Riley which was not so far away from Fort Leavenworth. Grierson made all the necessary arrangements, and soon, my great grandfather, Francis, and all his company men moved from Fort Leavenworth to Fort Riley.

Francis told Gramma Clara many times about how ecstatic the entire 10th Cavalry were when they received orders to depart Fort Leavenworth and move to Fort Riley. Francis would often tell her about how difficult it was for him and his army brothers to live in the miserable living conditions at Fort Leavenworth. They were often left without proper food, had no access to training facilities, lived on the cold swampy terrain with God knows what kind of creepy crawlers making nights miserable. Yet instead, none of them ever complained to Grierson or any of the seniors because every one of them was ready to give everything for their country.

My research and Gramma Clara's accounts tell us that the heroes of the 10th Cavalry had so much at stake while living and trying to survive at Fort Leavenworth. During rainy seasons, the whole swamp would overflow, flood their camps, displace all their belongings, and drenched the brave men facilities with thick swampy water. I can only imagine Francis being miserable and dissatisfied about living in those unbearable conditions but still staying strong, trying to keep himself from getting sick so that he could focus on his military training and duty. I can also imagine him standing up for his men against the cruelty of Hoffman. I learned that during one of the rainy seasons in June and July, an outbreak of

Cholera took many lives within the eight companies at Fort Leavenworth. Also, many of the patients later caught pneumonia due to the rainy, wet, and damp conditions that they had to endure and live in.

A lot of the infected men had to be quarantined. I recall Gramma Clara sharing with us that Francis was one of those unfortunate soldiers who caught pneumonia but thankfully, it wasn't serious. I can visualize him lying on the makeshift bed in the crowded medical camp on the swampy low land of Fort Leavenworth. It must have been so difficult, all isolated, seeing your brothers in pain, coughing, having breathing difficulty while the doctors try their best to make sure no one reaches critical condition. Francis took all these challenges head-on; He wanted to serve his country and live up to being the best soldier for the country. His aim was to represent the African American society to the best of his abilities without letting anything or anyone destroy his spirit and eagerness to serve his country and make it a more inclusive society for everyone, regardless of their race or creed.

The regiments received orders to move from Fort Leavenworth to Fort Riley on August 2nd, 1867. I am sure this was an exciting moment for all the troops. I can just imagine their jubilation, the rejoicing, the hand slapping high fives, celebrating their departure. Their pain and suffering were not going unnoticed, and their restationing showed that the government cared about them and their lives. The situation made it clear that the government wanted to make sure that their integrity and respect weren't hurt further. After a few preparations, the 10th departed Fort Leavenworth and made their way to Fort Riley, Kansas, on August 5th, 1867. However, Grierson had other plans for Company E, which was my great grandfather Francis' regiment, as they were not sent to Fort Riley but were ordered to make their way to Fort Arbuckle in Oklahoma for a special task.

Despite Francis' absence in Fort Riley, it is my duty to reflect upon the experience of the Buffalo Soldiers at the Fort because that's what Francis would want, to honor his brothers. Moreover, I want to document the Buffalo Soldiers' whole journey as accurately as possible.

On August 7th, 1867, all the other regiments except the 10th Cavalry finally arrived at their new home, Fort Riley. It would have been an exhausting journey for them, but I can just imagine how happy all of them were when they reached the fort. A place where they could have basic amenities of life and train with proper facilities. Grierson could finally execute all his plans he had developed for his regiments because he wouldn't have to deal with Hoffman's arrogance and

24

racism. He could finally train his soldiers the way he wanted and polish them into courageous, skillful, and honorable, brave men of the United States Army. Francis would've been overjoyed to learn that they now had adequate shelter for living and food to feed themselves, keeping their morals boosted. Speaking of food, this may have been one of the only garrisons where their regiment had adequate food to eat. Gramma Clara mentioned to us that Francis loved good food. One of his favorite dishes was a bowl of greens and cornbread. Moreover, Gramma also told us that her father enjoyed cooking as well. I can see how he would've loved to cook a pot of stew for his brothers at the Fort and make them drool over his culinary skills.

Everything at Fort Riley started moving in the right direction with Grierson in total command. My research shows that the soldiers were given proper shelter in quarters which they help build themselves. It must have been great for them to finally have access to all the resources they deserved; nice, warm, and comfortable beds, adequate amounts of food, and training facilities. I can only imagine how wonderful it would have been for Francis if he had been there but being assigned a special task to go to the Indian Territory for the United States Army only outweighs comfort. One can only imagine the trust and confidence that Grierson had in my great grandfathers' regiment to send 10th Cavalry, Troop E, on a special assignment to another state. I can bet that Francis would have been so proud and happy about this assignment.

Fort Riley holds significant importance in the history of the Cavalry. This is where the African American recruits were finally receiving the training they deserved under Grierson's tutelage. This is where the Cavalry was completed with the formation of the companies I, K, L, and M. It must've been a proud moment for the whole regiment to be finalized. Soon the soldiers were properly trained, skillful, and well-equipped soldiers of the US Army. These African American men made history, and each one of them deserves their stories to be heard and documented. Every time I think about Francis, I cannot narrate the sense of pride and patriotism I feel. I feel proud of being related to a National Hero who shed his blood and sweat in the line of duty.

However, at Fort Riley, things weren't always smooth. There were many battles and raids that occurred during this time, and it's essential to note how bravely each member of the Cavalry performed in these skirmishes. One specific incident that I would like to mention here is from the Pacific Railway route. In Early August 1867, P.S. Ashley and a crew of six men were surveying and preparing to construct the route for the Union Pacific Railway. They were attacked by 30 Cheyenne warriors, who wanted to stop them from constructing train tracks through their homeland. All of them were ruthlessly killed. However, one man, William Gould, survived and somehow managed to reach Fort Hays, Kansas. There, before succumbing to his wounds, Gould shared the tragedy with the army representatives, who then ordered a skirmish to take place to clear the region of the Cheyenne threat. Since Fort Hayes was responsible for the safety and protection of these railroad workers, they had to own up to the Cheyennes' terror. They called upon the 10th Cavalry situated at Fort Riley for support who sent their brave and highly skilled Company F, led by Captain George Armes, to the rescue. Had Francis been a part of this squad, I can assure you, he would have been the first one to prepare himself for battle. Honor, bravery and courage ran through his veins, he would have done all he could to protect his brothers and the people of this nation. Armes and his Cavalry moved northwest towards the Saline River. Although, they were in need of support from the Thirty-Eighth Infantry, in which they lost track of the 10th and returned back to Fort Riley with no hopes of finding the 10th's Company F. Company F was ambushed and attacked by around 400 fierce and well-equipped Cheyenne warriors at the Saline River trail. Armes, with his quick thinking, ordered his Company to dismount their horses and fight on foot. However, the outnumbered soldiers had nowhere to go as they were surrounded by ruthless Cheyenne warriors from all sides. I can visualize how despairing of a position they were in, knowing that one wrong move could end their whole skirmish. How difficult it would have been for them, knowing how the Natives could step up and slaughter each one of them in a flash. Despite all those thoughts, the soldiers kept their calm and followed Armes' orders. This shows how disciplined and brave each and every one of them was. Armes had so little time to think, but in the time of despair, he came up with a strategy that carried his men through. However, Armes was an intelligent commander, he ordered his men to form a "hollow square" around the horses and march toward Fort Hays which was 25 miles away. The Company slowly made their way to Fort Hays as they fought valiantly against the Cheyennes while also staying in their positions. As the soldiers approached closer to Fort Hays, the Cheyennes retreated since they knew they'd be walking straight into their death trap. Amazingly, despite the hopeless position the Cavalry was in, they made it to the Fort, and the casualties were very few. The only soldier that lost his life that day was Sergeant William Christy. This made Sergeant Christy the first martyr of the Cavalry. Learning about the death of Christy was probably a truth defining moment for the 10th. I can imagine Francis holding back his tears at the news of losing a brother in battle. I guess deep inside, they all knew what was at stake, but reality hits hard when it materializes.

Another battle involving the 10th during their time at Fort Riley was one of the deadliest battles, The Battle of Beecher Island, which is also known as the Battle of Arikaree Fork. The instigation was caused by the Cheyenne and Arapaho warriors since the railroad tracks continued to cross through their sacred lands. The warriors continued to raid, loot, and plunder the railroad workers throughout Western Kansas. General Philip Sheridan was the Commander of the army in the area. So, he decided to call upon the 10th Cavalry for support and to guard the area against future raids. Sheridan was outnumbered and didn't have enough troops under his command to fully patrol the area, which is why he had to recruit a group of 48 men to become scouts to identify where the Native Americans were stationed so that they could diffuse the threat as soon as possible.

On September 10th, 1868, news reached Fort Wallace that a train had been raided by Native warriors. In response to this, the scouts followed the trail to locate the raiders. However, they soon realized their numbers weren't enough to match against the quick and agile Native warriors. Therefore, the men camped for the evening near "Dry Fork near Republic River." The Native Indians, on finding out the location of the Scouts, planned a surprise attack at the brink of dawn. However, Forsyth, the leader of the scouts, identified a feathered silhouette firing his rifle. He managed to kill the Indian right on the spot. Hearing the shots, the scouts immediately woke up and prepared to face the attack of hundreds of Indians. The scouts took shelter on a sandbar in the middle of the Arikaree, from where they continued to shoot their rifles at the Indians. The Indians were surprised by the firepower and felt outmatched with their current strategies. So, they decided to reduce the effectiveness of the scout's power by waiting them out. The army scouts were surrounded on all sides and had limited supplies, they had nowhere to go and were stuck in Arikaree waiting for their imminent death. The battle continued for the next few days, and as a result, a number of Scouts were martyred, and many Indians died along with their tribal leaders. The scouts realized their only way out of this trap was to seek reinforcements. The problem for them was that the natives had surrounded their camp from all sides and were waiting for any movement from the soldiers to instigate an attack. So, stepping out in numbers wasn't an option. So, two to three of them sneaked out at midnight and made their way to Fort Wallace to seek help. In response, three different units of Cavalry, which included the brave and courageous Companies H and I of the 10th Cavalry, headed out to assist the scouts. On September 25th, they reached the hopeless, weak, and wounded scouts who were forced to survive on the decaying flesh of horses. This battle had to have been dreadful and frightening. Days of fighting without food and living in survival mode, in a way, I am glad to know that Francis wasn't a part of this event, but on the other hand, I believe that if he was, he would have been the one standing in front, fighting the natives for his brothers and country. The reinforcements successfully held off the Indians while saving the injured and dying scouts from their misery by safely escorting them back to Fort Wallace.

Apart from these deadly battles, the 10th was actively involved in patrolling and protecting workers and settlers as they continued to expand the development projects of the new era. Their efforts, valor, honor, and integrity continued to shine as they fought bravely in each battle and skirmish regardless of how outnumbered or outmatched they were. Their faith in their abilities, passion, and pride for their country, and their devotion to duties ensured that they were ready to fight till their last breath. Sometimes, they managed to amazingly overcome difficulties which to the eye may have looked completely impossible. Miraculously these soldiers displayed their courage, bravery, and successfulness as a regimental unit.

Despite Francis' absence at Fort Riley and its associated skirmishes and battles, it can be assured that the Buffalo Soldiers, all across, were a brave cohort of strong and fearless men. They were given a chance to serve and prove their abilities to those who stood against their recruitment. This wasn't just a fight for their country's honor, but it was also a fight to protect the whole African American community's honor. These men paved the way for the future enlisting's of African Americans in the army, they paved the way for integration across all sectors. It is because of those bold, brave men that we have the agency we possess today in present America.

After a commendable display of bravery and skillful combats at Fort Riley, four companies of the 10th and 6th were ordered to move to Fort Arbuckle in Oklahoma. At that time, Francis and his company E were already stationed at Fort Arbuckle rebuilding the fort and protecting the Kansas Pacific Railroad. So, Francis was once again reunited with his cavalry brothers. Now the 10th Cavalry and their journey of valor, commitment, and bravery continues on to the next garrison in Oklahoma – Fort Arbuckle!

"It was on the road to the future paved with the blood and sacrifice of Black Americans, that I became the first Black Chairman of Joint Chiefs of Staff."

- General Colin Powell

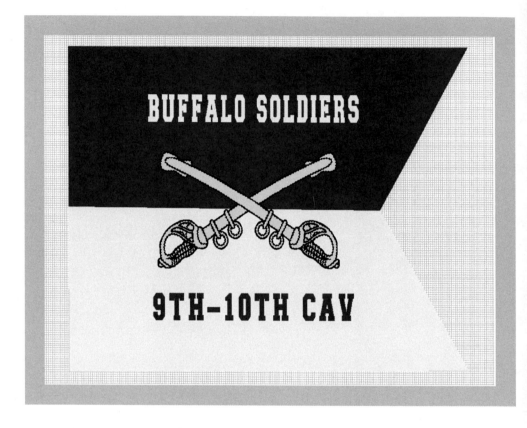

The Flag of the Buffalo Soldiers 9th and 10th Cavalry

Chapter 4: Fort Arbuckle (1868–1869)

Major General Philip Sheridan, Hancock's successor as commanding general of the Department of Missouri, ordered the 10th Cavalry to move to Fort Arbuckle. Philip instructed Grierson to move his headquarters from Fort Riley to Fort Arbuckle to scout the country to the west. The army wanted to establish a post in the heart of the recently settled Kiowa and Comanche reservation to keep things in control. The cavalry had already proved their bravery and efficiency against the Indian threat in the past. Again, the regiment was in charge of building and establishing this post, the army could easily observe the activities of the Indians and operate against them when necessary. So, Grierson left Fort Riley on May 1 with his adjutant, Samuel Woodward, the regimental chaplain, W. M. Grimes, and nineteen troopers. On his way there, he stopped at Fort Gibson only long enough to mount E and M Companies, and then they pushed on to Fort Arbuckle.

Four more companies of the 10th Cavalry joined the other regiments stationed at Fort Arbuckle in order to make the fort fully functional to protect the Union Pacific Railroad. The total number of soldiers enlisted at the fort, present and absent, amounted to 25 officers and 702 enlisted men as per the records. The companies were posted along the line of Union Pacific Railroad to protect the construction teams and act when necessary. The companies' ulterior motive was to stop the myriad, barbaric raids on Texas by the Indians.

Soon after the arrival of the 10th Cavalry and under the command of General Phillip Sheridan, Fort Arbuckle was reconstructed and started operating as a supply depot for the winter campaigns against the Comanche. As soon as the soldiers arrived at the fort, they were assigned their duties. Every single one of them was appointed tasks based on their skills, past experiences, and the fort needs. The troops did exactly as they were told, and the extent of their obedience and discipline nourished as they started to establish the fort to make it functional. Their tasks consisted of the same routine, building the barracks, taking care of the horses, maintaining the horse-feed warehouses, defending the Indians' attacks in the region, and they had to always be on constant guard. In addition to the fighting, they pursued the outlaws and cattle thieves, constructed roads, laid down telegraph lines, kept under surveillance the postal service, removed the illegal settlers, and kept trouble at bay. Apart from the daily tasks, the routine life of a trooper was dreary and consisted of hard work. Every day the troopers had to get up to the sound of their Commander at dawn, and after a light meal, they would get to work.

I can only imagine the discomfort and weariness it brought my great grandfather and his cavalry brothers, working as long as the daylight reigns with little to no escape from the work life. This type of labor-work regarding the army does bring a lot of empathy and honor to those who have never worked manual labor. Considering the back-breaking work, none of the soldiers ever gave up, they continued giving everything they had in the name of honor and duty.

I can picture in my mind clusters of troopers going on about their daily duties, working together under the surveillance of their commanding officer. Drops of sweat rolling down their muddy and dusty faces onto the uniforms bearing their unit's distinctive logo. The logo that they carried on their shoulders with pride and honor. The day's hard work consisted of cutting and collecting the material for building, working on maps, architectural designs, and constructing the fort with the little material that they were provided to work with. These troopers had to deal with the hardships that came with manual labor and the difficulties that the harsh weather of Oklahoma brought with it. Oklahoma's humidity and the consistent winds flowing in from the south or southwest, along with its dry arid, sub-tropical land, only made life and work miserable for the soldier's.

So, for the 10th Cavalry, there was almost little to no leisure time, and if there was any portion of the day that was considered spare time, it was the nighttime, which the groups spent enjoying the benefits of their steady pay. Most of which went to taverns. The troopers being away from their families, the distress of racial discrimination, the worry of losing one's life, the constant fear of the Indian war parties' attack, and the loneliness were all now too familiar with the standard Black cavalryman.

In order to seek solace, some of the soldiers drowned their sorrows and money in liquor. I often wondered how the alcohol affected these inebriated soldiers. Well, I can imagine them as they would start with their problems and sorrows and think about it all night long, some would start singing their regimental song or gospel hymns, and others would just drown in their sorrows only by drinking all alone. Due to racism, it made intoxication particularly dangerous for the troops of color. The white people thought of them as experimental, and charges of immorality could easily taint their reputations regarding such matters. In extreme intoxication cases, the determined punishment would be imposing a fine, which would not have decreased the intensity of inebriation that was prevailing.

I wondered how my great grandfather Francis must have dealt with all of this, along with the distress of being away from family. One can get lonely with all the hard work and having no one to share hardships and worries with could be depressing. My great grandfather Francis told my Gramma Clara that he used to send more than half of his paycheck back home rather than waste it away on foolish recreation. In my eyes, that made him a man of dignity, devotion and dedication. Rather than having to go on lackadaisical endeavors to take his mind off of reality, Francis truly stood his ground and refused to give in to the escapist mindset that prevailed in the rooms of Fort Arbuckle at night.

However, there were still some problems at Fort Arbuckle that needed to be managed. There was this eminent problem of poor sanitation and hygiene rendered upon troops, making them highly vulnerable to many diseases. With the arrival of the Cholera pandemic in the 1860s, poor sanitation problems made it even worse. Due to lack of proper laundry-equipment, many soiled clothes would end up as a stack in tents, which attracted flies and created a difficult situation for the troops. Moreover, it made ventilation difficult, and the flies would make anything and everything filthy. This went on for some time until the conditions started improving gradually with the arrival of fresh supplies and materials required for building permanent structures. Despite their risky duties, troopers had to receive medical help for pneumonia and other airborne diseases. Gastrointestinal diseases were particularly common at that time; almost a third of Black cavalrymen had to receive diarrhea treatment. Considering these health risks, it seems unimaginable to think of how they survived with all these diseases and the increased risk of catching them at any time. One can only imagine the paranoia that it would have created among the men at Fort Arbuckle.

After 1869, several new and old diseases spread worldwide across the globe and were contagious to groups with poor hygiene and sanitation. These included malaria, cholera, typhoid, and scurvy. These often kept the troops down and distressed. As tiring as their job was, the constant worry and fear of catching a contagious disease caused more anxiety among the troops. I can hardly imagine the dirty and poor conditions they had to live in before the barracks were built; living in poor quality tents, staying up all night because of the harsh weather conditions, running out of supplies often, having living spaces infested by insects, and poor ventilation, etc.

Along with the diseases and poor sanitation was the problem of diet. Sometimes the soldiers' diet was unhealthy. The quartermasters would fail in providing edible meat to the troopers. The meat would often be spoiled, doomed by the insects and flies that it attracted. This would lead to further unease in their digestive systems. It was indeed the case that the little food that they would get would almost always be rotten or spoiled. I find it unfathomable to live without the provisions we have today, only to imagine what misery this must have been for them. Yet they remained in their sphere of duty and only with the keenness to do well for their nation. For me again, this was in its own self a moment of pride for Francis and the Buffalo Soldiers. I feel mighty honored that I am a descendant to a Buffalo Soldier just thinking of their display of strength, character, and commitment to their duty.

Because the Buffalo Soldiers were stationed in Oklahoma, I must mention the Boomer movement that started around the 1860's. After the civil war, The U.S. Government had taken to making treaties with some of the Nation's Indian tribes that inhabited the lands, some of which had fought on the Confederacy's side. These tribes were namely Creek and Seminole tribes of the Indian territory. These two groups were forcibly removed from their lands and placed in Oklahoma, at that time known as the unassigned lands. Some groups of people tried to settle there and then came to be known as "Boomers." The U.S. Military attempted to remove as many boomers as possible during the civil war. These boomers worked as settlers for the Seminole and Creek groups; they took the land and tried to restore it themselves. Among the many duties of the Buffalo Soldiers instated in Fort Arbuckle, removing the boomers was added to the list. It seemed like the civil war was still going on despite the government's best efforts to make things better for both ends. But the rebellion of the American Indian tribes showed in the form of "boom" or "boomers," a term which was brought into existence by Dr. Morrison Munford of Kansas City, who had also written a paper on this matter. But now, the boomers were raiding, looting the settler houses, and plundering all the trains passing through. The Buffalo Soldiers had to stop this atrocity and lawlessness that the Boomers had instigated in the region. They were assigned the task of maintaining law and order in the area.

Laying down telegraph lines and protecting the postal service was another task assigned to them in order to keep the communication going. Hours of laborious work of digging, placing the lines, and then again solidifying the ground by putting back the soil on top of the place was consuming. It involved such hard work, diligence, and meticulousness. The troops had shown skillfulness not only on the battlefield but also in construction, following orders, and physical labor. Protection of the Postal Service required constant and persistent guarding, which, of course, did involve changing shifts over time.

Sheridan disliked the location of Fort Arbuckle and Fort Cobb as they were not situated in the right locale with respect to Kowa and Comanche reservation. Moreover, they were too far to afford adequate protection of the Texas frontier. He desired a new post to replace both Fort Arbuckle and Cobb. He discussed possible new sites with Colonel Benjamin Grierson. Grierson and his party went to Medicine Bluff on the morning of December 29 and inspected the new site and was impressed.

The clear, trickling water of Medicine Bluff and Cache Creeks assured a pure and ample supply of materials. Moreover, the whole area was covered by a rich carpet of grass, animals that could be hunted everywhere, and the Wichita Mountains' rugged beauty promised an abundance of building materials. He reported back the details of his inspection to Sheridan, who decided to move immediately to the new site and construct a permanent post. The departure date was set, and the Troops were ordered to finish up and finalize the Fort related assigned tasks.

While preparing to move to the new site, heavy rains delayed the departure for a week, and even then, the long column of troops and wagons had to slosh through a sea of mud and water to get to the new site. Swollen streams added to the difficulty, and four days passed before all the troops reached "Camp Wichita" their new site. The men set to work immediately erecting temporary shelters, the

10th troopers constructing their "homes" from condemned tentage, brush, and mud. They were facing difficulties as the supplies expected from Fort Arbuckle had not arrived because of the road's condition between that post and Camp Wichita. Grierson ordered his trustworthy unit, Captain George T. Robinson, and the men of Company E to construct the road. Francis Clinton and his fellow troop brothers put in the road between the posts. Working swiftly, the troopers threw a 135-foot bridge across Beaver Creek. My great grandfather and his cavalry brothers cleared trees, underbrush, and before long, they built a bridge and made a clearing for the road. By the end of February 1869, supplies were flowing without difficulty between Arbuckle and the new post.

Work began immediately at the new post. After dismantling an old sawmill at Fort Arbuckle and moving it to the new site, fatigue details of cutting logs in the Wichita Mountains, opening rock quarries, dressing the stone, and constructing quarters, stables, and storehouses were moving swiftly. This construction was back-breaking work, but the men worked as a team and successfully built the new post, Camp Wichita, later named Fort Sill!

Fort Arbuckle was strategically obsolete by 1869 when Fort Sill was constructed farther west. My research about my great grandfather Francis Clinton's life continues with his journey from one fort to another. This time it will be from Fort Arbuckle to Fort Sill. So, just like my great grandfather and his 10th cavalrymen would say, "READY AND FORWARD"! On to the next garrison, Fort Sill!

Chapter 5: Fort Sill (1869–1873)

Francis' story takes us to Fort Sill that lies amidst the dry lands and humid subtropical climate of Lawton, Oklahoma. Today Fort Sill serves as US Army Field Artillery School, Marine Corps' site for Field Artillery MOS School and US Defense Artillery School. It is also one of the four locations for Army basic combat training. Fort Sill United States Army Post is located north of Lawton, Oklahoma, about 85 miles southwest of Oklahoma City. It covers almost 94,000 acres which are about 38,000 hectares.

One of the remarkable stories that was passed down from generation to generation in our family was how Francis and his fellow Buffalo Soldiers helped build Fort Sill. It is indeed a great honor to know that my great grandfather was instrumental in building Fort Sill along with many of the other frontier posts. There was no better way to relive his memories than going to tour the fort.

The trip to Fort Sill in Lawton, Oklahoma, had been scheduled in advance. I had made arrangements for my family to tour the fort in March. This was around the time COVID-19 pandemic began to spread across the Nation, but we could not let that stop our mission. We were ready and determined to move forward with Francis' life story. My husband, Clarence James, and I had arranged to meet my sister and her husband, Sharon and Alvin Love, at Fort Sill Military Base. The plan was to meet up with them at the visitor's center and proceed to the post quadrangle to meet our tour guides and tour the facilities. Clarence and I left Garland, Texas, on the morning of March 10, 2020, and headed towards Lawton, Oklahoma. We journeyed to Fort Sill, crisscrossing the prairie states in search of the truth about Francis Clinton, my great grandfather. The drive was about three and a half-hour long, and it was stimulating to my imagination. The weather was magnificent, and the views were breathtakingly beautiful. It was a picture-perfect day! My mind wandered off during the ride, I envisioned my great grandfather with his Buffalo cavalrymen galloping across the plains on their horses, making a commute from one fort to the other. Always ready to protect and serve their country. All I could think of was how these men helped shape history for America, and how they need to be recognized for their contributions. I thought how bold, fearless, brave, and ambitious the heroic Buffalo Soldiers were back in the 1800's. The world needs to recognize that the Buffalo Soldiers helped build many of the forts and garrisons across the Western Frontier, including Fort Sill. I had to remind myself that I was going to see first-hand a magnificent accomplishment they helped achieve for this country. I was looking forward to visiting the post that my great grandfather Francis Clinton and his cavalry brothers built from the ground up. The place they called home and protected with their lives.

We arrived about 12 - noon and met Alvin and Sharon at the visitor's center. After exchanging small talk, we headed straight to the historic post quadrangle to meet our tour guides.

When we arrived, we were welcomed by our tour guides, Robert Anderson Jr., James C. O'Leary, and Kenneth Reese. They took us on a private and highly informative tour. We got the chance to visit many of the buildings at the historic post quadrangle. We were given the VIP treatment because they knew that Private Clinton helped build many of the structures at the fort. First, we toured the barracks where the troopers lived. Next, we visited the mess hall where the soldiers ate. Then we drove around the post quadrangle and saw the officer's house along with Sherman's house built by the Tenth Cavalry. I was taking it all in, but I could hardly wait to visit the historical guardhouse, as, for me, it had a lot of special memories attached to it. Based on the army return records that I received from Robert Anderson, Jr., I knew Private Francis Clinton served as a prison guard at Fort Sill on December 1871, February 1872, March 1872, and April 1872. These documents of his service were proof that my great grandfather served duty in the prison guardhouse over 100 years ago. My curiosity was pumped up, and I was eager to visit the historical prison that he helped build and served as a prison guard.

Finally, the tour guides told us that our next stop was the prison guardhouse, and I was so excited that my eyes lit up with joy. As we approached the guardhouse, I could hardly believe my eyes because it looked as if we had stepped back in time. The actual building from the 1800's was absolutely astonishing. The idea that Francis Clinton served as a guard here made me enthralled. When I walked into the building, it was a bit eerie, and I swear I could feel and sense my great grandfather's presence. The building was old and gloomy, with a moldy smell. I pictured my great grandfather standing in the guardhouse door with his rifle in his hand and great big proud grin on his face for serving in the United States Army. The experience was more extraordinary than I had actually imagined, just knowing that he guarded prisoners here in the 1800's was amazing. On the first floor, we saw the jail cells where the prisoners were held. Mr. Anderson and Mr. Reese took us upstairs to the sleeping quarters where the guards slept when they spent the night on duty. I sat on one of the bunkbeds and could not stop thinking, "My great grandfather slept here. This is hard to believe that my great grandfather slept here!" I was in awe at the organization of it all. How the rifles and shackles were on the wall, and the beds were neatly arranged in the room. I marveled looking at the engineering and construction of all the buildings at Fort Sill, especially the guardhouse. My respect and esteem for Francis and the 10th cavalry increased even more. They stood together to create such a beautiful place that stands tall and magnificent to this day. I could not hold myself back, and at that moment, tears of joy ran down my face. This was a huge moment for me, and I felt as if I had just made an incredibly special and lasting bond with my great grandfather, Francis Clinton.

Mr. Anderson and Mr. Reese had a wealth of knowledge about the Buffalo Soldiers and what their life was like at Fort Sill. We learned so much about the fort, how the buildings were built, where the officers' lived, where the Indian reservation was located, and now, we were ready to visit the museum and take in every bit of information that they had to offer. We toured the museum that was built in order to commemorate the brilliance and determination of the Buffalo Soldiers. The museum held remnants of that specific time period. I walked inside and came across the walls decorated with pictures of the men at work formed into clusters performing their assigned tasks as if it were routine. Inside a glass showcase, there were weapons and equipment that were actually used by Francis and other Buffalo Soldiers. Every single item kept in the museum spoke highly of the accomplishments of the 10th Cavalry. Looking at all of those items made me relive the memories of the Buffalo Soldiers and how they helped the government marshals, accompanied stagecoaches, wagon trains, and laborers, watched railroad development etc. I could imagine them removing Boomers, pursuing burglars, catching horse thieves and cow rustlers, and giving security to Native Indians in the Indian Territory. The two things in the museum that captured my attention the most were the life-size statue of a Buffalo Soldier with his horse and the table model of early Fort Sill with the Indian reservations and the historic post quadrangle. I was able to visualize what life was like for Francis and the Buffalo Soldiers, their daily routine, their work ethics, and their drive to be the best regiment ever. As I stood at the table looking at the model of early Fort Sill with the Indian reservation and the historic post quadrangle; I began to form a mental image in my mind of what life was like at Fort Sill for the soldiers. I looked at the table with the model of the miniature sculptures of early Fort Sill and noticed that the Indian reservations were located nearby the historic post quadrangle. Seeing this set-up made me drift off into deep thoughts about an incident I read about that happened at Fort Sill involving one of the 10th cavalrymen.

My thoughts took me back to what I had learned about why the fort was built in the first place and some of the skirmishes and battles that the Buffalo Soldiers fought. One important fact that I learned was that Major General Phillip Sheridan was to lead a campaign into Indian Territory to stop the barbaric looting and raids carried out by the Native Indians against the people of Texas. Therefore, to stop the Indians, Major General Phillip Sheridan ordered six cavalry regiments accompanied by frontier scouts such as Buffalo Bill Cody, Wild Bill Hickok, Ben Clark, and Jack Stilwell to assist in the campaigns. My great grandfather's cavalry was one of the regiments that took part in the skirmishes on the order of Maj. General Phillip Sheridan.

From the start, the post was designated "Camp Wichita" and was alluded to by the Indians as "the Soldier House at Medicine Bluffs." Sheridan later named it Fort Sill to pay tribute to his West Point colleague and companion, Brigadier General Joshua W. Ledge. The major post leader was Brevet Maj. Gen. Benjamin Grierson, and the principal Indian operator was Colonel Albert Gallatin Boone, grandson of Daniel Boone. With the establishment of Fort Sill, the US army was strengthened significantly. It gave a boost to many wars and skirmishes on the frontier, helping United States Army regain control of the unassigned lands. Units from Fort Sill battled on the Great Plains in 1869 and in the Red River Wars of 1874–75.

While looking at the model of the post and Indian reservations on the table, I could envision that one particular incident that happened at the fort. In August 1869, the name of the new post was changed from 'Camp Wichita' to Fort Sill, and Private Benjamin Kewconda of 10th Cavalry Company E, one of my great grandfather's cavalry brothers, celebrated the event by becoming extremely intoxicated and disorderly in an Indian camp close to the post. He was apprehended for being intoxicated. When he was arrested, he yelled out offensive, obscene profanities to Grierson and all the officials of the Tenth. He was disciplined cruelly as per the laws of the Army. The brutal discipline in the military implied the trooper was seated on the ground, tied up with knees elevated, feet level, and arms bound to the front. A stick was then pushed over his arms and under his knees, leaving him totally powerless, and a bit of wood was generally utilized as a gag in his mouth. Ordinarily, such discipline kept going about a large portion of a day. Since Grierson ran a "dry" post, Kewconda's punishment was a bit extreme. It was a horrible incident, but it was necessary to maintain ethics and discipline in the Fort. Sergeant Gibbs also of Company E found more barrels of whisky buried outside the post, and ownership was traced to a few teamsters with four wagon trains. Grierson had the barrel kegs broken up, and the men with the wagon trains were escorted to Van Buren, Arkansas, for trail.

Another fascinating artifact at the museum that captured my attention and left me in awe, as I already mentioned, was the life-size Buffalo Soldier statue with his horse. As I reached out and touched the reins of the horse, standing by the life-size Buffalo Soldier statue, my mind went back to the story my mother and Gramma Clara use to tell us about Francis fighting on the Washita River. I imagined him holding tight to the reins of his horse while he was fighting the Indians in a skirmish on the Washita River. Yet, I envisioned the scenario of him falling from his horse, getting injured, but still standing up to take the traitors head-on. My imagination took me back to what I learned about some of the skirmishes and battles that my great grandfather and his Company E troops fought in. I learned that he fought in the Battle of Anadarko without giving up, holding the nation's crest on his chest.

As I mentioned, a bit about the Washita River incident and the Battle of Anadarko, I would like to describe in detail more about the history of the battle. Col. J. W. Davidson oversaw the 10th Cavalry, and he was aware of war parties raiding more along the Texas boondocks frequently, and they were occupied with killing. Davidson kept his troopers on consistent scout and quest for the warriors. The Comanche assaulted a wood camp almost twelve miles from Fort Sill. A unit of the exhausted Tenth showed up to deny the hostiles of 52 head of newly taken stock and to recover who had been killed and scalped.

Davidson ordered a command for more mounted force and gave this accompanying general request:

HEADQUARTERS POST OF FORT SILL

July 17, 1874

General Orders No. 46

The hostile bands of Comanche's, Cheyenne's, and Kiowa's, having committed depredations and murder upon government employees within the Reservation, and within a few miles of the Post, some marked line must be drawn between the hostile and friendly portions of those tribes. In order then that troops and others may be able to distinguish those who are friendly—all such Indians must form their camps on the east side of Cache Creek at points selected by the Agent.

No Indian hereafter will be permitted to approach this post nearer than the Agency, and with a messenger from the Agent stating the Chief and the number of his party.

J. W. Davidson

Lieut. Col. 10th Cavalry

Bvt. Maj. General USA

Davidson received orders on July 26 to proceed immediately with an enrollment of the Indians called "friendlies" at Fort Sill. Within the next few days, conditions at Anadarko got unstable. Some Kiowas killed six men in two days near Fort Sill. A lot of the Indians, dreading armed force reprisal, left the agency and joined the hostiles under Lone Wolf. The day when the only person manning the post was Captain Gaines Lawson, Commander of Company I, Twenty-fifth Infantry, the trouble erupted. Lawson sent Connell for reinforcement. That evening reinforcement was there with Troops from Companies C, E, H, and L under Captains Charles Viele, George T. Robinson, Louis H. Carpenter, and Captain Thomas Little were armed, mounted, and prepared to march. Davidson led them out of the post and set out quickly toward Anadarko.

Next Afternoon, Davidson crossed the Washita and entered the agency grounds. Chief Big Red Food was ordered by Davidson to surrender, turn over their weapons and move back to Fort Sill as prisoners of war. This did not go over well with the chief as an argument developed between the two, and Chief Big Red Food escaped into the bush. A battle started with the Indians trying to escape up the Washita River.

Davidson ended up in an awkward position. The Indians were retreating into the bushes, and the US Troops had no answer for them. Davidson did not want to harm any of the natives so, he hesitated to open fire on them. However, as his troopers pushed ahead, Kiowa warriors, who had taken position behind the commissary and corral, fired into the troops from the back, injuring Sergeant Lewis Mack of Company H and Private Adam Cork of Company E. A few horses were also hit. This is where I visualize my great grandfather falling from his horse and getting injured. Davidson, after swerving his command, moved abruptly into the thick timber along the Washita River and dismounted to fight on foot. Skipper Little with L Company moved out and drove the Kiowas from the store and corral into the plains where it was easier for Army to suppress their attack. Most of these Indians, be that as it may, surrounded Little's correct flank, crossed the waterway, and set out toward a ranch and the home of a Delaware named Black Beaver. Woodworker with his H Company sought after these Indians, charging and steering them to a weaker position. However, not before they had executed four men who were in the fields cutting feed and two more close to Black Beaver's home. During the night, Davidson posted troops at Shirley's, the grocery store, the office, and in the cornfield. These troops were assigned the patrolling and the scouting tasks. On the other hand, other troops demolished the camp of

Big Red Food and burrowed channels on the south side of the waterway. There was no retaliation from the Indian side all night, and that was an alarming situation for Davidson and the Regiments. It was the calm before the storm as by early morning, almost 300 Indians had assembled to recapture the bluff and started to climb the hill. Skipper Carpenter took E, H, and L Companies to face the Indian advance and managed to defeat the enemy troops. Frustrated, the Indians set fire to the dry grass in an effort to torch the agency. The troopers lit counter fires, and with much difficult work, the buildings and structures were spared.

The "fire battle" continued for a while but finished the clash of Anadarko. Davidson had four troopers and six horses injured. He suspected that fourteen Indians had been "shot off their horses," and at any rate, four horses had been executed.

I was always curious about how my great grandfather was injured and what battle he was fighting in when he got injured. Through my research, I was able to connect the dots and discovered he was injured in the Battle of Anadarko. This was the battle on Washita River that my great grandfather, Francis Clinton, spoke about a lot in his stories. When he fell from his horse, he ruptured his side but kept right on fighting the battle until the end. As soon as the battle finished, he was treated by the medical officers. He was kept under care for only a short period for his injury and returned to work duties as soon as he recovered. The injury from Washita River became a lifelong medical condition for Francis as it instigated health issues to his body. What is heroic about that accident is how he never gave up his will and remained steadfast in his mission of serving in the military till the end.

The other skirmish my great grandfather participated in is what I refer to as the Porch Skirmish. Let's imagine the moment together. On Saturday, May 27, 1871, the Kiowas came to the Indian agency in Fort Sill. Lawrie Tatum, the Indian agent for the Kiowas and Comanches, called the chiefs into his office to ask them about the Indian raid on the Warren Wagon Train known as the Salt Creek Massacre. He wanted to inquire about the person or the agency involved in the raid. Satanta, one of the tribal leaders, stood up, looked Tatum in the face, and boasted and bragged about how he led the raid with Chief Satank, Eagle Heart, Big Tree, and Big Bow. Tatum sent a detailed report to Grierson to inform him about the incident. He asked Grierson to take action against the guilty Indians.

Tatum then went to see Grierson and Sherman. They called a council meeting on the porch in front of Grierson's house so they could take action against the guilty Indians. Swift orders were issued to the Buffalo Soldiers to get mounted for the ambush against the raiders. The companies were stationed in a strategic position to prevent the escape of the Indians. A dozen troopers were already stationed inside Grierson's house hidden behind the shuttered windows facing the porch. Chief Satanta arrived because he had heard that one of the high-ranked Washington officers was on the post. When Sherman confronted him for his involvement in the raid, he tried to change the story and walk to his horse. When Grierson saw that, he drew his pistol and ordered Satanta to sit down, and he obeyed. He had no other option because he knew he could not outrun the Cavalry at that time. Chief Satank arrived with about twenty Kiowas to the council meeting a few moments later.

Sherman told them that the guilty chiefs were under arrest and would be sent to Texas for a court-trial. Satanta was enraged at hearing this and held up a revolver directly towards the commanding officers. Sherman, who already had his men armed, gave the command and the shuttered windows flew open with a dozen Buffalo Soldiers with carbines cocked and aimed at Satanta. He knew that he was in a compromised situation, and one pull of his trigger might lead to a bloodbath. So, he settled down. Another signal was given, and the stable gates opened wide, making way for the D Company led by R.H.Pratt. The company emerged into position in line on the left of Grierson's quarters. In the meanwhile, Robinson's company E, which my great grandfather was a part of, formed a detachment of two and blocked all the possible escape routes. There was no escape for the Indians on the porch. Lieutenant L. H. Orleman took his detachment quietly into position across the parade ground and behind the large body of Indians gathered to watch the proceedings on the porch.

At this point, Lone Wolf, Big Tree, and several others rode up to the council. Lone Wolf dismounted, carrying two Spencer repeaters, a bow, and a quiver full of arrows. As he walked toward the porch, he tossed the bow and arrows to one of the warriors, a carbine to another, and pointed a fully cocked repeater at Sherman. This created tension in the council. Grierson knew that, so, he kept his cool and carried on with the dealings. He grabbed Lone Wolf's carbine and, at the same time told Horace Jones, the Indian interpreter, to tell the Indians that violence would not save their chiefs. The Indians agreed and dispersed. Satanta and Satank quietly followed the orders and were escorted to the guardhouse and put in shackles. See, this is what I call heroic. That is the group of Buffalo Soldiers that I deem as awesome, brilliantly brave, courageous, and forever outstanding.

Preparations were made to return the Indian prisoners to Fort Richardson in Jacksboro, Texas. On June 4, two wagons were escorted to the guardhouse, and the cursing, kicking, and struggling Satank was forced into one of the wagons. It was guarded by a corporal and two privates because Satank posed a threat. Satanta and Big Tree got into the second wagon, with one trooper watching each of them. The column set out for Fort Richardson. What followed was mentioned in this letter Grierson's young son Charles wrote to his aunt.

Fort Sill, June 9, 1871

Dear Aunt:

Yesterday General Mackezie's command left here with the Indian prisoners for Texas. Satank said that he was not going to Texas at all, that he was going to kill somebody. He attempted to put his threat into execution by stabbing the corporal that was sitting in the wagon with him, and he was shot 3 or 4 places. When the soldiers were shooting at Satank, some of them shot the teamster, making a long wound on the head. The other Indians made no fuss at all. Today Captain Robinson is going to the mouth of Cache Creek with the remainder of his Company E (my great grandfathers' troop).

Affectionately yours,

C. H. Grierson

Now, let's get ready and explore the rest of Francis' story at Fort Richardson in Jacksboro, Texas.

"If given the opportunity, we as Black people can excel to the highest of heights."

-Clarence James Jr

Archietta Burch James in Front of Guardhouse

Archietta with the Statue of Buffalo Soldier

Layout of the Fort with Indian Settlements

Report of a Guard mounted at _Fort Sill I.T._, on the _22nd_, and relieved on the _23rd day of April 1872_.

Parole.							Articles in Charge.														Received the foregoing Articles
Countersign. _New Orleans_	Lieutenants	Sergeants	Corporals	Musicians	Privates	Total															
Detail	1	2	4	1	28	36															

LIST OF THE GUARD.

			Reliefs, and when Posted.						Where Posted.	Remarks.
	FIRST RELIEF. From 9 to 11 and 3 to 5			**SECOND RELIEF.** From 11 to 1 and 5 to 7			**THIRD RELIEF.** From 1 to 3 and 7 to 9			
No.	NAME.	CO.	REGT.	NAME.	CO.	REGT.	NAME.	CO.	REGT.		
1	Jackson	H		Bass	L		Jones	M		Quarter's Q House	
2	Smith	"		Jackson	9		Johnson	"		River "	
3	Sawyer	"		Alexander	L		Battes	"		Com & Mag'n	
4	Warden	L		Allen	9		Porter	E		Hay Yard	
5	Allen	H		Daniels	9		Jones	"		Q.M. Corral	
6	Brown	A		Kerg	"		Clark	"		C.O. Stable	
7	Fuller	L		Marshall	9		Brown	"		Hospital	
8	Wright	"		Beans	"		Clinton	"		Ind. Camp	
9	Waller	"		Johnson	M		Kelly	"		" "	

Sergeants } Mathews "M", Davis "A",   Corporals } Bright "H", Wallace "M", Hawkins "E", Coleman "L",
Orderly for _____ Officer of the way Eldridge "H",   _____   Bugler, Coleman "L".

LIST OF PRISONERS.

Note.—Name first the Prisoners under sentence by G.C.M., commencing with those who have longest to be confined.

			CONFINED.			SENTENCE		Sentence.	Remarks.
No.	Names.	Co.	Regt.	When	By whom.	Charges.	Com. mencing	Expires		

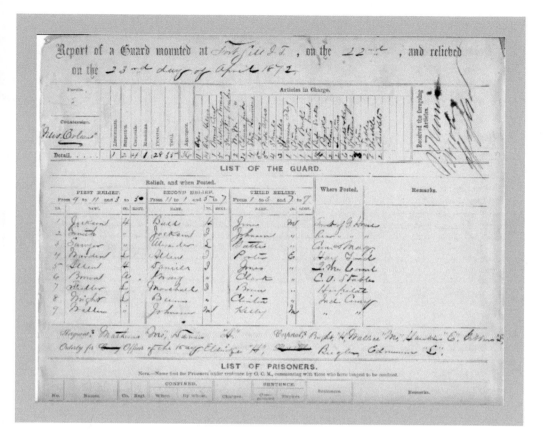

Guard Duty Details – 2

Proof of Origin of Disability.

This blank should be used by a Commissioned Officer, if possible; but if not possible to secure such evidence then the testimony of two Comrades must be obtained. See instructions on the other side.

State of _Kansas_ County of _Leavenworth_ ,ss:

In the matter of the pension claim of _Francis Clinton_
late of Co _F_ 10 Reg't _U.S. Cav_ Vols., personally

appeared before me, _Notary Public_ in and for the County and State

aforesaid _Wallace Thompson_ of _National Mil. Home_ in

the County of _Leavenworth_ and State of _Kansas_ , who

being duly sworn declares that his age is _40_ years; that he is the identical person who served as a

✓ in Company _F_ 10 Regiment _U.S. Cav_ Volunteers

and know the above named soldier, who was a member of Company _F_ 10 Regiment

U.S. Cav Volunteers, That on or about the day of _March_

18_74_ , while in the line of duty, and without any fault or improper conduct on his part, at or near

white on the Wachita River in the State of _Indian Territory_

said soldier incurred _Constipation from improper diet, bad water &c in camp & in field — and said trouble brought on a rupture of his right side from which he suffered, I know, thereafter, until his discharge and afterwards — When he was discharged from the army he was to my knowledge suffering from rupture of right side_

Affiant knows the above facts from being associated intimately with said soldier & claimant & being his friend while in the service as stated, and from having seen his rupture of the right side when he received it, and after his discharge from the army

✗

Dead —

Affiant further declares that he has no interest, direct or indirect, in this claim, and that he makes the

Chapter 6: Fort Richardson and Fort Griffin (1873–1875)

W hen I decided to write the book about Francis Clinton and the great Buffalo Soldiers, I had planned to visit every single Fort where my great grandfather served. So, in November 2019, my family traveling crew decided we would visit Fort Richardson in Jacksboro, Texas. The plan was simple, we decided that all of us would meet up in Little Elm, Texas, at my youngest brother's house and then leave for Fort Richardson after we were well-rested. So following our planned itinerary, we reached Sam's house and spent the night there with his wife Khan and their baby Bentley Blu Burch. On the morning of November 25, 2019, my sister and her husband Sharon and Alvin Love, my brother Vernal Williams and I set out for Fort Richardson, eager to continue our quest of unveiling the true history of an unsung and unrecognized Buffalo Soldier, Francis Clinton, our great grandfather.

While on our way towards Fort Richardson, we talked about what life must have been like for our great grandfather. We drifted into memories of the 10th Cavalry and our great grandfather. I was just sitting with my head on the car window, thinking about how Francis would have felt, moving across the plains of Texas, traveling from one Fort to another while facing fierce enemies. I imagined a group of Buffalo Soldiers marching towards the enemy in their battle positions, crushing down any foe in their path. I was in the world of imagination when a sudden thought provoked me, and I said out loud, "How would you feel if you saw a herd of buffalo roaming these Great Plains today?" For the next few moments, there was complete silence, and I could hear the air swirling in the

Great Plains. We imagined large herds of buffaloes grazing the Great Plains just like in the 1800s. We were discussing that when my brother came up with a question, asking what happened to the buffaloes of the Great Plains? I told him that according to my research, the government had plans to undermine the Plain's Indian way of life with the systematic slaughter of the animals. This decimated the vast southern herds in Great Plains by the time the first railroad was constructed and started operating. Just imagine after the buffalo hunters killed hundreds of buffalo, their dead decaying bodies were scattered across the plains. Did you know the buffalo bones that littered the region helped bring up the eastern trade market where the bones were sold? This was eased by the train system that followed. So, the government was able to kill two birds with one stone, but the main strategy was to slaughter the food source of the Plain's Indians and drive them onto government reservations.

The Army, without hesitation, carried on with its arrangement to obliterate the Indians lifestyle. Comanches, Kiowas, and Kiowa Apaches reacted to this strategic attack with assaults on settlements, wagon trains, and troop developments. They started kidnapping people and taking their horses and supplies. Troopers positioned at frontier posts dispatched a tireless military mission, leading to the Red River War of 1874-75, which in the long run constrained the state's last Native Americans onto reservations.

After the stimulating lesson about the buffaloes, we finally arrived in Jacksboro, Texas, where we had a pre-scheduled tour of Fort Richardson.

We met our tour guide, and he escorted us through the various buildings such as enlisted soldiers' barracks, post-hospital, the dead house/morgue, and the Officer's Quarters. He started telling us more about the Fort as we walked through the walkway into the world of memories of our great grandfather.

We spent about five hours at Fort Richardson gathering information about Private Francis Clinton. Fort Richardson, with very few buildings left, has now been converted into a state park. During the tour, the most fascinating part was when we came across one of the oldest Pecan trees in the region. The tree was in front of the Officer's Quarters, facing the parade grounds. The tour guide informed us that the pecan tree is one of the oldest trees in Texas, about 150 years old. As soon as I laid eyes upon it, I realized that my great grandfather must have eaten pecans from this tree during his time here at Fort Richardson. I walked closer to it and started searching the ground for pecans. Luckily, I spotted some and reached down to pick them up. I was lucky to find pecans still on the ground, but then I remembered that pecans were plentiful this time of the year. Now, I had another task at hand, and that was to crack the pecan open, and fortunately, I managed to do that. Just as I tasted one, I felt as if, in some way, the time had flashed back, and I was in the same era as Francis. For a brief moment, I imagined being with Francis and his fellow 10th cavalrymen, sitting under the same pecan tree, gathering pecans, talking about life, their families, and enjoying the beauty of the Texas afternoon. It was as if his presence still lingered here. We were instantly connected, once again. It gave me a sense of pride, to share the same blood, to be where he once was when serving the country with his utmost loyalty and devotion. I was so overjoyed that I even packed some pecans to take back home and preserve them in a treasure chest. These pecans were to serve as a memoir for my visit to Fort Richardson in Jacksboro, Texas.

Before heading back home to Dallas, we stopped at the visitor's center, and I learned:

Fort Richardson was among the most significant of the Federal Forts established in Texas after the civil war. At the time of the fort's establishment in 1867, the frontier situation was critical. Increasing raids by Comanches, Kiowas, and Kiowa Apaches had all but depopulated the northwestern frontier of Texas and had seriously threatened the entire westward settlement. Fort Richardson, only 70 miles from the Indian Territory (Oklahoma), occupied a highly strategic position in the line of frontier posts, created to meet the desperate needs of travelers and settlers.

In the spring of 1873, companies of the 10th were transferred to several Texas Forts; they were dispersed to Fort Richardson, Fort Griffin, and Fort Concho. The 10th Cavalry of United States, along with several other regiments, was stationed at Fort Richardson. The soldiers maintained the post, helped local law officers keep the peace, chased the criminals, escorted wagon trains, oversaw elections, protected cattle herds, and most importantly, patrolled for Indians.

During the Red River War 1874-75, Fort Richardson served as a major staging base for the columns of cavalry and infantry that swept the plains and inflicted final military defeat on the Comanche and Kiowa Indians.

For the next eleven years, Fort Richardson soldiers carried out the purpose of their military life. The primary hindrance to their activities was the Quaker Peace Policy, initiated by President U.S. Grant in 1869, which placed the Indian reservations under civilian control and prohibited military movements on the reservations. The tribes took advantage of this policy by raiding into Texas and returning to the sanctuary of the reservation, knowing that Troops from Fort Richardson could not cross the Red River in pursuit. Consequently, settlers continued to be harassed by Indian raids.

In response to the settler's complaints, routine patrols were dispatched almost every week. Soldiers, including my great grandfather Francis Clinton, guarded the military road connecting Fort Richardson with Fort Griffin and Fort Concho to the southwest to stop any kind of violence. Moreover, they provided escorts for mail and supply trains to move along the vital routes in greater safety.

The following is a detailed account of the Warren Wagon Train Raid or Salt Creek Massacre mentioned in the previous chapter. This incident and the battle of the Little Wichita River were the two most dramatic events to occur at Fort Richardson. A wagon train, owned by Warren and DuBose of Weatherford, Texas, was carrying corn on a government contract from Jacksboro to Fort Griffin, was attacked May 18, 1871. The attack occurred on Salt Creek Prairie, about 22 miles from Fort Richardson. A large force of Kiowas led by Chiefs Satanta, Satank, and Big Tree killed the wagon master and six teamsters and managed to wound five people.

General William T. Sherman was at Fort Richardson when one of the survivors, Tom Brazeal, brought the tragic news. Gen. Sherman and his escort had passed over the same spot the previous day. The Indians were massed there at the time, eager to attack, and were restrained only by the prophecy of the medicine man, Do-Ha-Te (owl prophet), he said that the second party to pass would be more easily captured.

Understandably alarmed by his narrow escape, Sherman (who had previously been skeptical about the Indian atrocities on the frontier) ordered Colonel MacKenzie to assemble four companies of his Fourth Cavalry and two companies from Fort Griffin for an all-out pursuit of the raiders. They were easily identified because Santana boasted about the raid to Lawrie Tatum, the Indian agent at Fort Sill, and named Satank and Big Tree as co-leaders of the attack. The chiefs were arrested in a tension-filled confrontation with Sherman at Fort Sill.

While enroute to Fort Richardson under the guard of MacKenzie and his forces, Satank was killed, attempting to escape. Satanta and Big Tree were later questioned for murder in the courthouse at Jacksboro. They were found guilty and, as a result, were put on a death sentence. Their sentences, however, were commuted to life imprisonment at Huntsville by Governor Edmund J. Davis, who later granted them parole in 1873. Though, both chiefs violated their paroles by leading raids into Texas. Satanta was arrested again in 1875 and returned to Huntsville, where he died because of falling from the first floor of the jail. As for Big Tree, he was arrested in 1875 but released at the request of federal officials. Thereafter, he kept his parole and died in 1929 in Anadarko, Oklahoma.

This particular Salt Creek Massacre was significant for two major reasons. First, General Sherman's close brush with disaster convinced him to take a much harsher stance on Indian Policies. Sherman was to be commander of the Army for the next 12 years, so it was his policies that were dominant during our Nation's Indian Wars. Secondly, the Indian Chiefs responsible for the murders were tried under the white man's law in the white man's court. The trial in Jacksboro was the first of its kind in Texas and one of the few Indian trials to have occurred in the United States. Indian leaders now realized that they would be held accountable for their actions and that they couldn't return to their safe establishments after a raid. After those trials, the Indian atrocities ended in the region for good.

In July 1874, President Grant revoked the Quaker Peace Policy, releasing the military to take measures against hostiles and their hostilities. Within three months, this new policy proved successful. On September 28, 1874, Colonel MacKenzie ended the Indian domination of the Southern Plains at the Battle of Palo Duro Canyon. By 1875, the frontier of Texas was relatively secure, and the services of the troops at Fort Richardson were no longer needed. Orders for the abandonment of Fort Richardson were issued March 29, 1878; on May 23, the last troops marched to their new stations at Fort Griffin. Fort Richardson's colorful and useful life as a military installation had ended.

At various times, Buffalo Soldiers of the 9th and 10th Cavalry Regiments served at virtually every Texas frontier fort from the Rio Grande to the Red River and onto the Panhandle. Francis Clinton served at Fort Griffin at various times during his service. Life as a soldier at Fort Griffin during the 1870s was typically a monotonous routine. Whether you served in the cavalry or the infantry— "life at the fort was always the same i.e., drill, reveille, mounting guard, retreat, calling tattoo and taps, hoisting the flag at sunrise and taking it down again at sunset." Life in the field was often preferred, but when it became overwhelming, and the soldiers were tired and worn out, they were happy to return to the mundane life at the post. Routine labor for the soldiers included working on buildings, maintaining fort roads, hauling water, gathering firewood, tending the post garden, and bringing lumber to the fort from the steam-powered sawmill on Mill Creek. The hardest fatigue duty at Fort Griffin was the task of operating the steam sawmill.

The proud Black Troops built and renovated dozens of forts, strung thousands of miles of telegraph lines, and escorted wagon trains, stagecoaches, railroad trains, cattle herds, railroad crews, and surveying parties. They opened new roads and mapped vast areas of the West. They recovered thousands of head of stolen livestock for civilians, brought dozens of horse thieves to justice, and pursued Indian raiders, often having to stay on the move for months at a time. No matter what they did to settle the western frontier, they were never credited for it. There was friction between civilians and the Black Troops. Texas, of course, was, after all, a former slave-holding state. So, any face in a blue uniform was resented and hated.

"I Don't Think Any Rough Rider Will Ever Forget the Tie That Binds Us to the 9th And 10th Cavalries"

-Theodore Roosevelt

Pecan tree in front of Officer's Quarters facing the parade grounds

Pecans from the Tree

Indian Chief Satank

Indian Chief Satanta

Chapter 7: Fort Concho (1875– 1883)

"The truth is the truth — the bible says the truth shall set you free and this country needs the truth."

- Archietta Burch James

Fort Concho in San Angelo, Texas, is where Francis Clinton's military career as a Buffalo Soldier ended, and my quest for unveiling the true story of my great grandfather's life began. I heard my mother and Gramma Clara speak so highly about him throughout my childhood, and I wanted to know more about his life. I was dedicated and committed to searching for the truth about my great grandfather, the unsung Buffalo soldier. I was concerned about how and where to start writing this book; what to and not to present to my readers, to tell you the truth. To be honest, I was actually clueless until I received the Divine intuition. God spoke to me in a vision and showed me the path to take. He wanted me to follow the footsteps of Francis, traveling to prominent military garrisons and ships where he served while in the United States military. Whether or not you believe that it was God's way of speaking to me in a dream about how to start writing the true story about my great grandfather, I know it was God's intervention. I could not have written this book without God's guidance and direction. My vision was precise, detailing for me to travel to the important posts where Francis served, research, and tour the garrisons/forts and ships. Following His guidance, I started at Fort Concho in San Angelo, Texas, and began working my way backwards. Due to the global pandemic I had to visit the last two bases virtually. When the pandemic is over, I plan to visit Fort Leavenworth in Kansas and his first military establishment, the Historical Naval Ship in Baltimore, Maryland. I had a rough idea given to me through my dream, but it still needed a lot of refinement, and the only way to do this was through proper research. So, I started doing my research, unveiling and exploring Francis' life timeline in search of my answers.

My sister Sharon Love, her husband Alvin Love, and I started our journey searching for the truth about Francis Clinton on October 17, 2019. We started this journey by visiting Fort Concho in San Angelo, Texas, where he spent the last years of his service. We knew he was one of the famous original Buffalo Soldiers that played a vital role in settling the American Frontier. We were determined to see how Francis Clinton helped win the war for the United States as a Buffalo Soldier by retracing his magnificent journey. As we drove many miles across the great state of Texas, my heart pounded with excitement because I knew I would be unveiling history about an unsung hero. Remember, the game plan was to work our way through Francis Clinton's career timeline from the last garrison to the first naval base in Baltimore, Maryland. While we traveled to San Angelo, Texas, from Garland, Texas, we could not help but admire the scenic countryside. The vast fields stretched as far as we could see. The farther south we drove, the more we noticed the cotton fields spread across like little white clouds on both sides of the highway. My sister reminded us that these cotton plantations were filled with Black Slaves harvesting cotton for their white masters just over a century ago. Over the years and with the constant effort of people like our great grandfather, the scenario has changed, African Americans started getting the recognition they deserved. We realize it was a struggle, and we still have a long way to go. I am trying to get Francis Clinton and the Buffalo Soldiers the credit they deserve for what they've achieved for this country. What a surreal feeling! We all got quiet and took in the moment. We didn't say much until we reached Fort Concho in San Angelo.

I had a scheduled a 1 hour 30 minutes private tour of the garrison and museum for the descendants of Private Francis Clinton a Buffalo Soldier of the 10th Cavalry, Company E, that served at Fort Concho around 1875-1883.

When we arrived at Fort Concho, we were greeted by a welcoming staff. They treated us like royalty because, according to them, they rarely had visitors that were living descendants of the famous Buffalo Soldiers. They were impressed with our extensive knowledge of our great grandfather, Francis Clinton, and asked us to share every detail that we could to help them with their research.

The staff at Fort Concho was accommodating and knowledgeable. They shared so many stories about the Buffalo Soldiers and their lifestyle while at Fort Concho with us. We learned so much about what life was like during the eight-year period Francis served as a Buffalo Soldier at the Post. Based on some of their stories and my research, life was exciting but extremely difficult at Fort Concho for the soldiers. According to our information, research and background history of the Post:

Fort Concho served as regimental headquarters for the Tenth Cavalry, known as the Buffalo Soldiers, from 1875 until 1883. Grierson and his "Buffalo Soldiers" arrived at Fort Concho on 17th April 1875 and established the regimental headquarters. The 10th Cavalry took up the duties that the 4th Cavalry previously held, i.e., patrolling the frontier, escorting stagecoaches, wagons and settlers, cattle drives, railroad survey parties, and mounting expeditions. Francis, along with the other Soldiers from Fort Concho, scouted and mapped large portions of West Texas, built roads and telegraph lines. The 10th Cavalry scouted 34,420 miles of uncharted terrain, opened more than 300 miles of new roads, and laid over 200 miles of telegraph lines. These feats were accomplished while having to be constantly on the alert for hit-and-run raids of Apaches. The 10th played an essential role in the 1879-1880 campaign against Chief Victorio and his renegade band of Apaches. The Buffalo Soldiers, along with Francis, stayed in pursuit of Victorio for several years.

Victorio began three years of raiding in Mexico, Texas, and New Mexico. In Texas, he raided mostly between Fort Davis and El Paso and occasionally headed south to Mexico. He was pursued in Texas by United States Army troopers of the Black Ninth Cavalry, commanded by Col. Edward Hatch, and the Black troopers of the Tenth Cavalry, commanded by Lt. Col. Benjamin H. Grierson. The Tenth Cavalry was stationed at Fort Concho, near the site of present-day San Angelo, but was transferred temporarily to Fort Davis to assist in the final campaigns against Victorio. During Grierson's first foray into the region, he led his troopers on a 1,500-mile march searching for the Apache leader. He returned to Fort Concho on May 20, 1880, so his men could rest before resuming the chase. In July, he was ordered back into the field south of Fort Davis. In this campaign, he received assistance from troopers at Fort Quitman, New Mexico, as well.

During most of the summer of 1880, Victorio camped at various sites Quitman, Carrizo, and Guadalupe mountains of far western Texas. When Grierson heard early in August that Victorio was headed north from the Rio

Grande toward the Guadalupe Mountains, he led troopers in that direction, keeping the mountains between his position and that of the Indians. Grierson decided to change his strategy in confronting Victorio. Instead of his men chasing Victorio across the desolate countryside, he decided to ambush Victorio by posting his men at the canyon passes and water holes he thought the Apache chief would use. He hoped to spring a trap near the watering-place Rattlesnake Springs. They set their trap and waited for Victorio to pass by. Fortunately, they found themselves in luck that day. Grierson's troopers successfully confronted the Apaches at this location, where they fought a three-hour battle before the Indians fled westward into Carrizo Mountains and on to Mexico. Grierson men chased the retreating Apaches as far as they could. However, Victorio and his apache warriors manage to escape that day but were destroyed later, October 15, 1880, by Mexican soldiers under the command of Colonel Joaquin Terrazas.

It was during the hard-driven chase of Victorio when my grandfather Francis contracted frostbitten toes. Records indicate he was admitted to Fort Concho Post Hospital on November 18, 1880, with frostbitten toes on his left foot. This was an act of God that he was in the Post hospital; because my research indicates that during this time some of his cavalry brothers were mercilessly killed in San Angelo.

The city of San Angelo had quite a reputation for such a small town over the river near the fort. It had a collection of saloons and brothel houses. The enlisted men spent much of their time – and money – in the town, but its inhabitants were not appreciative of the Black Soldiers. San Angelo was one of the most hostile and racist environments for Black Soldiers. The residents repeatedly insulted, menaced, and harassed the Black Buffalo Soldiers. Around about 1880-81, tensions between the town and the Fort Concho garrison were high. Late in January 1881, an incident happened that made the soldiers furious and fighting mad with the town citizens of San Angelo. The soldiers sometimes danced or sang for drinks in the saloons, and on the night of January 31, 1881, Private William Watkins of Tenth Cavalry, Company E was mercilessly murdered while engaged at McDonald's Saloon. Tom McCarthy, a sheep man on the San Saba River, was enjoying the show and buying drinks. When Watkins finally tired and expressed a desire to stop, McCarthy insisted that he continue. Watkins protested politely, but this was enough to offend McCarthy. He pulled his pistol and killed the unarmed trooper with a shot through the head. McCarthy fled the saloon, but he was apprehended by post guards at Fort Concho on his way out of town. He was held until the following morning when he was released in the custody of Sheriff Jim Spears. Instead of jailing the prisoner, Spears permitted him the town's freedom, pending an examining trial. Feelings ran high at the garrison, and on Thursday, February 3, 1881, this notice appeared on the streets of San Angelo:

Fort Concho, Texas, Feb. 3, 1881

We, the soldiers of the U.S. Army, do hereby warn the first and last time all citizens and cowboys, etc., of San Angelo and vicinity to recognize our right of way as just and peaceable men. If we do not receive justice and fair play, which we must have, someone will suffer if not the guilty, the innocent.

"It has gone too far, justice or death."

SIGNED U.S. SOLDIERS

Their rage knew no bounds, and a large number of troopers armed themselves marched into town and relieved their feelings by firing into several buildings, including the Nimitz Hotel. According to the local sources, more than 150 shots were fired, although no one was killed and only one man was slightly wounded. The troopers dispersed quickly when bugle calls and the roll of drums from the post indicated Grierson was preparing to send a sufficient force into town to preserve order.

During Tom McCarthy's trial for Watkin's murder in Austin, Texas, he was found "not guilty." That was a perfect demonstration of White Supremacy, Judicial and Systemic racism that the United States underwent in the post-civil war.

Not long after that, another Black soldier was murdered. On the night of February 19, 1881, Private Hiram E. Pinder of Company F, 16th Infantry, was murdered in the town of San Angelo by a citizen without any cause or provocation whatever, and the murderer was furnished with a fast horse by the citizens of the city, allowing the culprit to escape and get away, which he did. So, another murderer of a US soldier managed to escape the law and not get arrested.

Since I have researched actual incidents, this is another incident worth mentioning:

This incident involves a Texas Ranger. In 1877, the arrival of a few Texas Rangers brought severe trouble to San Angelo and the Black Troops. Several Texas Rangers were visiting the Nasworth saloon to drink and dance and discovered that many Black troopers were doing likewise, at which point they pulled their six-shooters and pistol-whipped the soldiers. When the incident was reported at the post in Fort Concho, Grierson asked the ranger Captain John S. Sparks, for an apology, and instead, he responded that the little Texas Ranger company could whip the entire Fort Concho garrison. Fortunately for all concerned, Grierson's temper was unpredictable.

However, the affair did not end well, for the angry troopers armed themselves, went back to Nasworth's saloon, and shot up the place, killing an innocent bystander. Responsibility for this unfortunate turn of events pointed squarely on Captain Sparks, and he had to resign from the Texas Rangers service.

These stories had my head spinning and my mind wandering, but we were not finished with the stories, because we were headed to meet the historical librarian. We had scheduled an interview with the historical librarian/archivist during our visit to Fort Concho, and she was accommodating. I am so thankful to her because she not only provided us with Francis' historical army return records, she gave us some critical information to ponder. The interview was very enlightening and informative. She was deeply knowledgeable and knew a lot about that era and the Buffalo Soldiers. She said something that perturbed me about how the government portrayed the Black Buffalo Soldiers. One thing I noticed right away was that she kept referring to the Buffalo Soldiers as the governmental experiment (this I had to fact check and do more research). She also said the Black Buffalo Soldiers were not mentioned in history because, as far as the government was concerned, their existence and names didn't matter much. This was disturbing for me and caused me a significant bit of anxiety. I wanted to fact-check all of her information and do my own research before coming to a conclusion. I wasn't going to give up just because someone said there were no names associated with the Buffalo Soldiers, and their names didn't exist. I was determined more than ever to attach the name Francis Clinton with the Famous Buffalo Soldiers and American History. So, that day the title of my book was created, and it is: "Francis Clinton, a Buffalo Soldier and American Hero." My unwavering will to write the true story of Francis Clinton and the famous Buffalo Soldiers was real!

What an eventful day it had already been, and now we were ready to tour more buildings at Fort Concho. It was mesmerizing when I visited the school/chapel where the Buffalo Soldiers attended classes and were taught how to read and write. Grierson insisted that all his soldiers learn how to read and write, in which I was elated. While touring the school, I went to the front of the classroom to take pictures, and the teacher in me came out, and before I realized it, I was pretending to be the soldiers' teacher instructing the class. This moment made me feel proud, because I am a reading specialist and to know that Francis and the Buffalo Soldiers learned how to read and write was awesome. What a lifetime accomplishment for the soldiers!

We continued our tour of the facilities by visiting the post-hospital. This was a very surreal moment for us when we saw the cot Francis had to lay on when he was admitted to the post-hospital for frostbitten toes on his foot. I could only imagine the pain he suffered when he was in the Post hospital on November 18, 1880, for frosted feet while chasing Victorio.

On a lighter note, the tour guide had saved the best part of our tour for last. We were heading to the barracks or the living quarters where 10th Cavalry, Troop E, lived. Barrack 5 - was where Francis stayed and spent most of his time living with his cavalry brothers.

We were chauffeured around the Fort in a golf cart, and I remember being so excited as our golf cart pulled up in front of Barrack 5! I had my camera and iPad ready to snap pictures and video the precious moment. The minute I set foot inside the barracks was magnificent. I got goosebumps all over my body. I felt light-headed, like I would faint, but I was not about to destroy this magical moment. I was so excited that I couldn't help but grab my sister's hand and said, "are you feeling what I'm feeling in this marvelous moment?" "This is our great grandfather Francis' barracks where he lived, slept, and spent so much time during his service here at Fort Concho." We took pictures and videos of everything that we saw in the barrack, from the floor to the ceiling, everything that once was in use by the Buffalo Soldiers. The same floor that we were standing on was where he once treaded. Unbelievable! I felt he was actually there in the barracks with us, smiling and happy that we would keep his legacy alive. I could feel his spirit everywhere as I moved throughout the barracks. I did not want to leave. So, we just kept walking around until the tour guide said, let's go around back to the mess hall to see where the soldiers ate and dined. When I stepped outside of his barracks onto the walkway that led to the mess hall, I imagined Francis walking on the walkway with me, his arms around my shoulders, telling me that he was so

69

glad that I was keeping his legacy alive, and he had been waiting for this moment. I felt ecstatic and knew that I had to get his story out to the world.

The world needs to know his name and the outstanding contributions Private Francis Clinton and the Buffalo Soldiers accomplished in settling the Western Frontier for America.

Private Francis Clinton was honorably discharged from the United States of America Military, Tenth Cavalry, Company E, as a famous Buffalo Soldier on February 2, 1883 and moved to Oklahoma. Let's explore his life in Oklahoma.

Barrack 5 Buffalo Soldiers 10th Cavalry Company E Quarters

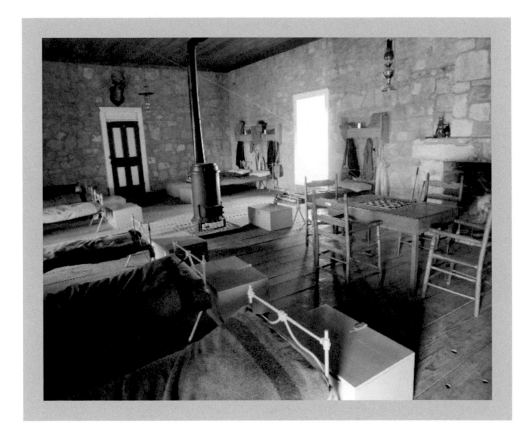

Inside of Barrack 5 where the Buffalo Soldiers Stayed

Mess Hall where the Buffalo Soldiers dined

School where Buffalo Soldiers learned to read and write

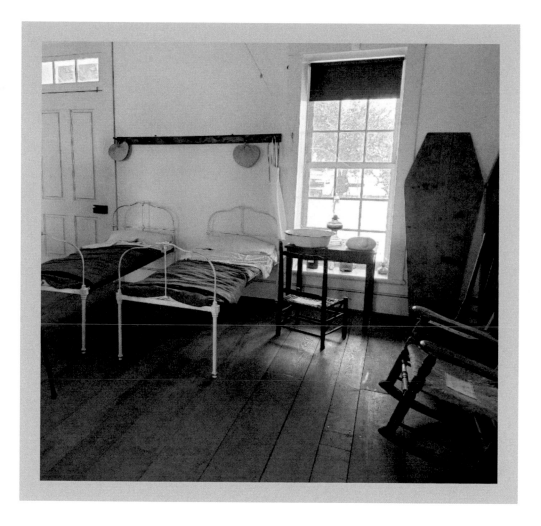

Fort Concho Hospital

Victorio, Apache Chief

WAR DEPARTMENT,

SURGEON GENERAL'S OFFICE,

RECORD AND PENSION DIVISION.

Washington, D. C., _____ *May 21,* 188*5.*

To the Adjutant General, U. S. Army.

Sir: I have the honor to return herewith the papers received from your office in pension claim No. *536252.* , with such information as is furnished by records filed in this Office, viz: that *Pvt. Francis Clinton, C. C, 10" U. S. Cav. was admitted to Post Hosp. Ft Concho, Tex Dec 8/80 with Frost bite of toes of left foot, and returned to duty Feb 28/81, remarks: Agu 26, in line of duty Nov 17/80.*

To return of the 10" U. S. Cav. (for C. C.) on file showing treatment.

By order of the Surgeon General:

No. *347616.*

per *JSB*

B. F. Pope
Assistant Surgeon, U. S. Army.

(171)

Fort Concho Report on Frost Bitten Toes

War Department,

ADJUTANT GENERAL'S OFFICE,

Washington, D.C. May 23, 1885

Respectfully returned to the Commr. of Pensions. Francis Clinton enlisted on the 21st day of May, 1867, and was assigned to Co. "E" "10" of U.S. Cavalry. Discharged May 21st ___ by expiration of service. A private.

Again enlisted in the same organization, Feby. 3, 1873 and was discharged February 3, 1878, by expiration of service. A private.

Re-enlisted in the same organization, Feby. 3, 1878 and on the muster roll for Nov. & Dec. 1880, he is reported present sick in hospital since Nov. 18, 1880 — "frosted feet" contracted in line of duty — station of command, Fort Concho, Texas. He was discharged February 2, 1883, by expiration of service. A private.

Under the enlistment of Feby. 3, 1878, he is reported for duty on all rolls other than the one quoted.

Report of the Surgeon

Gen'l ___

RECEIVED
JUL 22 1891
A.G.O.
W.D.

O.D. Greene
Assistant Adjutant General.

By ___

Detail Report of Francis' Duty and Hospital Stay

Chapter 8: The Oklahoma Land Run (1889)

After Private Francis Clinton completed his military service and retired from the 10th Cavalry, Company E of the United States Military Services as a Buffalo Soldier, he moved to Oklahoma and staked out a land claim. He ran in the last land run for the family property near Langston, Oklahoma. This is how the family claimed ownership of our homestead that we call the "farm" today.

A homestead is a plot of land, ordinarily, 160 sections of land were granted to any US resident who swore to settle and cultivate the land for five years. The main point was that the candidate must be at least 21 years old (or be the head of a family) and should have never "borne arms against the United States Government or given guide and solace to its enemies." With the section of the Fourteenth Amendment, which promised US citizenship to African Americans and ex-slaves, homesteading turned into an opportunity for the newly freed people. Soon after that, President Abraham Lincoln signed the Homestead Act of 1862, which allowed settlers to claim lots of up to 160 acres provided that they lived on the land and improved it.

Furthermore, after a Supreme Court choice in 1898, outsiders were qualified to apply for a property, too. However, at that point, the best grounds had just been asserted. From 1862 to 1934, the government conceded over a million and a half residences to private residents. This spoke to roughly a modest amount of the whole landmass of the United States. It was a gigantic exchange of land possession from the government to singular residents and introduced a progression of "land surges," during which homesteaders hurried in to settle the land on "the early bird gets the worm" premise. The Homestead Act encouraged the fast settlement of regions in the West and Midwest United States.

By the 1890s, improved farming and farming methods drove some white Americans to understand that the Indian Territory land could be important, and they forced the US government to permit white settlement in the area. In 1889, President Benjamin Harrison concurred, making the first of a long arrangement of approvals that inevitably eliminated the vast majority of Indian Territory from Indian control.

The Unassigned Lands were considered some of the best unoccupied public lands in the United States. The Indian Appropriations Act of 1889 was passed and signed into law with an amendment by Illinois Representative William McKendree Springer that authorized President Benjamin Harrison to open the two million acres for settlement.

The Oklahoma Land Rush of 1889 was the first land rush into the Unassigned Lands. The area that was opened to settlement included all or part of Canadian, Cleveland, Kingfisher, Logan, Oklahoma, and Payne Counties of the United States of Oklahoma.

At decisively noon, a great many would-be pilgrims made a frantic race into the recently opened Oklahoma Territory to guarantee modest land. The 2,000,000 sections of land opened up to white settlement were situated in Indian territory, an enormous zone that once incorporated a lot of advanced Oklahoma. At first, viewed as unsatisfactory for white colonization, Indian Territory was believed to be an ideal spot to migrate for the Native Americans who were taken out from their customary grounds to clear a path for white settlement. The movement started in 1817, and by the 1880's, Indian Territory was another home to an assortment of Indian tribes, including Chickasaw, Choctaw, Cherokee, Creek, Cheyenne, Comanche, and Apache. Oklahoma had a total of seven land runs at that time. The initial and most famous Land Rush was of April 22, 1889, which gave rise to the terms "Eighty-niner" (a veteran of that run) and "Sooner."

Another monumental event that took place during that time was named the Exodus of 1879. As Jim Crow isolation got settled in the South during Reconstruction, racial brutality and the unavoidable suppression of African Americans established a hostile environment.

The Exodus of 1879 was the primary mass movement of African Americans from the South after the Civil War. These transients, the vast majority of the previous slaves, became famously known as Exodusters, a name that took motivation from the scriptural Exodus. During which Moses drove the Hebrews out of subjection in Egypt and into the Promised Land. The Exodusters got comfortable with the conditions of Colorado, Kansas, and Oklahoma. Kansas was viewed as an encouraging place with a fresh chance to succeed because it had contended energetically for its status as a free state. Also, the western migration of African Americans during the Exoduster movement established all-black towns in the Indian Territory.

One attempt to make Oklahoma a Black state was to appoint Edward Preston McCabe as governor of the Oklahoma Territory. The authorities believed that it would make it easier for Black families to settle within the region during the land rush. This plan fell through the cracks, as there seemed to be less excitement of migrating to the new land, and instead, McCabe had to settle down as a treasurer in Logan County of Oklahoma.

With the history being set, I think I can move on with the story of my family. My great grandfather's duties as a Buffalo Soldier of having to escort settlers from the unoccupied public lands educated him about the land runs. After his retirement from the Military services, he was prepared and ready to participate in the last land run. The Land Run of 1895 was the smallest and last run in the state of Oklahoma. It came about with an agreement between the Kickapoo Indians and the federal government. According to the agreement, individual Kickapoos' 22,640 acres of land was to be sectioned for the land run. The land run opened 6,097 plots of 160 acres of former reservation land. The land run occurred on May 23, 1895, in central Oklahoma, west of the Indian Meridian.

Francis Clinton was honorably discharged in 1883 after a service in the military's 10th Cavalry with the symbolic name given to him and his brothers of the 10th Cavalry, the Buffalo Soldiers. After serving almost two decades in the military, his career defined his life and character. He had learned a lot from his service in the United States military and gave back everything that he had to his country and his duty. Due to his astuteness and insightfulness, my great grandfather took advantage of the opportunity to partake in Oklahoma's last land run. Ingenious, as I would think him to be. During the Land Rush, it was a growing belief within the African Amcrican community that this opening of free land was their opportunity to create communities of their own without the influence of racism. Across the nation, prospective settlers began hitching their teams to wagons and loading aboard their families and scant worldly goods. Others saddled their fastest horses or caught trains for what they considered to be the most advantageous point of entry.

On May 23, 1895, at 12 o'clock noon, it was the time for the last Oklahoma land run. I can almost imagine the whole scenario, and I want all of my readers to envision it with me. I imagine the blast of the gunshot echoing into the surrounding area as Francis gives a whirl to the reins of his horse. He rides in the whirlwind of dust, riding as fast as the wind with his stake in hand to stake out his claim on our homestead. Francis was a member of the 10th cavalry, so he was well trained in riding a horse. That day, he rode forward with zeal and zest until he spotted his land to claim, and he staked out 160 acres of land in Logan County near Langston, Oklahoma. He was indeed ready and searching to start a new life. A life he rightfully deserved after spending almost two decades in the military services, scavenging off scraps in the unruly and harsh terrains and living on survival mode.

He had learned so much from his military years about being his own man, riding, mapping out the land, constructing structures, and farming. Now, he was ready to settle down, find a wife and a homestead. Not long after the land run, he settled down and found the love of his life, Charlotte Tipkins. Francis and Charlotte Tipkins Clinton were married on April 14, 1897. To this beautiful union, seven children were born. On February 14, 1898, Clara Clinton (my grandmother) was born. She had six brothers and sisters: Cora Clinton, Samuel Clinton, Cleo Clinton, Blanch Clinton, Emmitt Clinton, and Verna Clinton.

Francis Clinton lived a life of valor, courage, commitment, dedication, and loyalty. He gave every bit of his life to the country he called his home. As a navy sailor to a member of the famous Buffalo Soldiers, Francis lived the life of a hero in the United States and died as a patriot of the country. Francis, my great grandfather, and the unsung Buffalo Soldier, finally left this world on March 25, 1917. Charlotte, his dear wife, lived a life, raising his children with the same love for the country and empathy towards society. She died on April 3, 1937.

"Do not get lost in a sea of despair. Be hopeful, be optimistic. Our struggle is not the struggle of a day, a week, a month or a year, it is the struggle of a lifetime.Never ever be afraid to make some noise and get in good trouble, necessary trouble."
- Rep. John Lewis

Charlotte and Francis Clinton

Marriage Certificate

Beaulah Land Cemetery Langston, Oklahoma

Charlotte Clinton

Francis Clinton

Buried at Beaulah Land in Langston, Oklahoma

THE UNITED STATES OF AMERICA,

To all to whom these presents shall come, Greeting:

Homestead Certificate No. _____
Application _____

Whereas, There has been deposited in the General Land Office of the United States a Certificate of the Register of the Land Office at _____ Oklahoma Territory, whereby it appears that pursuant to the Act of Congress approved 20th May, 1862, "To secure Homesteads to actual Settlers on the Public Domain," and the acts supplemental thereto, the claim of _____ Francis Clinton _____ has been established and duly consummated, in conformity to law, for the _____

according to the Official Plat of the survey of the said land, returned to the General Land Office by the Surveyor General;

Now know ye, That there is, therefore, granted by the United States unto the said _____ the tract of land above described, to have and to hold the said tract of land, with the appurtenances thereof, unto the said _____ and to _____ heirs and assigns forever.

In Testimony Whereof, I, _____ Grover Cleveland _____ President of the United States of America, have caused these letters to be made Patent and the Seal of the General Land Office to be hereunto affixed.

Given under my hand, at the City of Washington, the _____ day of _____ November, in the year of our Lord one thousand eight hundred and _____ Ninety-five, and of the Independence of the United States the one hundred and _____ twentieth.

BY THE PRESIDENT _____ Grover Cleveland

By _____ Secretary
_____ Recorder of the General Land Office

Recorded, Vol. 3, Page 279

UNITED STATES
TO
_____ Francis Clinton

Territory of Oklahoma,
_____ County. } ss.

This instrument was filed for record on the _____ day of _____ A. D. 189_, at _____ o'clock _____ M., and duly recorded in Book _____ of _____ at Pages _____

_____ Register of Deeds

Homestead Contract

86

Indian Meridian Monument - was the starting point for 1895 Land Run

Long Description:

Located on the northeast corner of Indian Meridian Road and W. Washington Ave., on the east side of Langston, you will first be startled and amazed at the 15 ft. tall obelisk in the middle of the road....but that's another Waymark.

This historical marker is a white/gray granite marker with an engraving of a settler's horse-drawn wagon at the top. The inscription reads:

"INDIAN MERIDIAN / Surveyed by E. N. Darling / Texas to Kansas - 1870 / East is Iowa Indian Reservation settled Sept. 22, 1891 / West is Unassigned Lands settled Apr. 22, 1889 / All farms, town lots, oil wells in Oklahoma east of the Panhandle are designated from Indian Meridian and Base Line. Main road Guthrie to Stillwater early 1890. Monument erected Apr. 1922 on proposed Ozark Trail. Original plaque erected 1967 / Replacement erected 2013." Beneath that are the names of the Major Sponsors of the marker.

Chapter 9: A Tribute Honoring an American Hero – Francis Clinton, the Buffalo Soldier

I'm just a Buffalo Soldier

In the heart of America

Stolen from Africa, brought to America

Said he was fighting on arrival

Fighting for Survival

Said he was a Buffalo Soldier

Win the war for America

-Bob Marley

After touring the numerous forts/posts/garrisons and researching for the true life story of Francis Clinton, my great grandfather, I have to say the very least, that I have immense pride and honor for him as an American hero. As the story unfolded, I learned more about the role Francis and the Buffalo Soldiers played in shaping America that should have been told in history but was never told. You are probable wondering why I keep repeating their story, well it's because it is worthy of repeating. It's an untold part of American History. The

89

proud Black Troops built and renovated dozens of forts, strung thousands of miles of telegraph lines, and escorted wagon trains, stagecoaches, railroad trains, cattle herds, railroad crews, and surveying parties.They opened new roads and mapped vast areas of the West. They recovered thousands of head of stolen livestock for civilians, brought dozens of horse thieves to justice, and pursued Indian raiders, often having to stay on the move for months at a time. No matter what they did to settle the western frontier, they were never credited for it. There was friction between civilians and the Black Troops. It is appalling to me that even after many years of service, they are still rarely mentioned in the history books and stories. Francis Clinton served in the U. S. Navy and the 10th Cavalry Company E as one of the famous Buffalo Soldiers for nearly two decades and no one knows his name. Of course, I believe it is my duty to bring remembrance, acknowledgment, and honor of him and the Buffalo Soldiers to the American people. Francis Clinton and the Buffalo Soldiers not only made the American dream possible for so many people, but they paved the way and open doors for many to follow. The Buffalo Soldiers exhibited bravery and valor on many occasions and lived a shining example of fraternity with their cavalry brothers, and that made them exceptional and successful. Despite the turmoil that was brought upon them, they stuck together to get the job done and looked out for one another in the time of need, just as a brother would do. Francis was a brave and fearless trooper who prioritized duty and order first. He took to heart the teachings of the military. Through his hard work and painstaking efforts, he left behind a legacy that will live on forever in this book and in the hearts of people. He was appreciated on countless occasions for his heroic service and was considered by his Commander, Colonel Benjamin Grierson, among the best he had trained, according to my Gramma Clara. She once told us an account where Francis mentioned how his sacrifices, bravery, and acumen had been admired by Colonel Benjamin Grierson. What I remember about it is that he said, "Trooper Clinton has shown immerse bravery through trial, and test of time and even the adversities he faced, he turned out to be an outstanding, polished soldier, with his abilities, and skillset that made Company E shine among the others. Indeed, the bravery of Francis Clinton is remarkable and praiseworthy. He has proved from time to time, that he is a worthy asset and an essential member of the 10th Cavalry… In short, he deserves the name Buffalo Soldier American Hero." Gramma Clara beamed with pride when she recalled that remarkable memory of my great grandfather. One could tell the sense of pride she had in her eyes and the immense respect she had for her father, Francis Clinton. Another story Gramma

Clara told us was how Francis raved about how sometimes his fellow troopers would lose their spirits on certain occasions, especially during the times of battles. At those times, Francis would boost their morale and remind them of their mission and their purpose in serving the United States of America. It takes a true soldier to fight battles, but it takes a leader to hold his brothers' heads high so that they can, with absolute courage and faith, fight for their country. Francis Clinton was indeed a true hero and patriot.

A great piece of history had been lost until now and had never been told or taught to the world. I firmly believe that this is an integral part of history, which has been left out of our school curriculum, more so from history itself as if it had never happened. Let us not forget the struggle and great endurance of these brave men. The impact my great grandfather, Francis Clinton, and the Buffalo Soldiers, had on the History of America should be remembered. It is my mission to bring this history to light and, in turn, lighten the path with the truth about the Buffalo Soldiers by narrating my great grandfather's struggles, hardships, and his great perseverance. It should be established in the school curriculum so that school children can learn about the accomplishments of our great Buffalo Soldiers. This book will not only contribute to the academic curriculum of America's youth, but it will forever remain in the History of America as a shining story that thousands will take inspiration from. As his great-granddaughter and an educator, I will advocate and push to get more stories about the Buffalo Soldiers into the school curriculum. I feel the school system failed me as a child because I was denied the right to learn about the Buffalo Soldiers' great chapter of American history. As a matter of fact, in February 2019, my granddaughter Jaylah James had a school assignment to create a report on her favorite Black History Hero. Jaylah asked her teacher if she could do her report on her great-great-grandfather Francis Clinton a Buffalo Soldier. She told the teacher that her grandmother Archietta (Gee Gee) was writing a book about him. The teacher thought it was an excellent idea! About two weeks into working on her report/project, Jaylah called me disappointed. She said, "Gee Gee, do not be upset, but I can't do my report on great-great-grandfather Francis Clinton, the Buffalo Soldier." I enquired, "Why not?" She said there is not enough information or books in our school library on the Buffalo Soldiers. Jaylah said, "The requirements are I must have at least (2) two resources for the report, and there is only one book in the school library on Buffalo Soldiers." I said, "oh no, we must fix that problem." (Houston, we got a problem---America, we have a problem) I am dedicated to finishing this book and donating a copy to Jaylah's school library. Hopefully, the next African American student or any student who wants to do a report or project on the Buffalo Soldiers will be able to do so. Her school will have more than one book available on Buffalo Soldiers in the library. This is one reason I am so committed to making sure our children learn the truth about these brave Black soldiers that helped shape the Western Frontier. My granddaughter has every right to know that her great-great-grandfather was an American hero.

Jaylah has been extremely excited and interested in the Buffalo Soldiers and Francis Clinton because her father, John James, has taken her to the Buffalo Soldier Museum in Houston, Texas, on several occasions. She knew he was assisting his mother (Archietta) with researching the Buffalo Soldiers while she was working on her book project. She was so impressed with the Buffalo Soldiers and what she was learning about her great-great-grandfather Francis Clinton that she wanted to know more about him and the Buffalo Soldiers.

Again, as Francis Clinton's great-granddaughter, I advocate for his honor, respect, integrity, and legacy to not be forgotten by promoting this book about his life and the Buffalo Soldiers. I was not able to read about his accomplishments in school as a child, but hopefully, his other descendants will have the privilege of learning about him and the famous Buffalo Soldiers. I feel a sense of pride that my lineage connects me with such a valiant and gallant man's bloodline.

He has earned the right to be added to the history books, to receive the Congressional Medal of Honor and a Historical Marker on his gravesite.

My incredible great grandfather, Francis Clinton, invested most of his energy and time serving in Company E of the Tenth Cavalry Regiment for the United States of America. The Tenth Cavalry was formed in 1866 in Fort Leavenworth, Kansas, under the order of Colonel Benjamin Grierson. Colonel Grierson had looked to enroll just the most prepared and educated officials in his regiment; the greater part of these men were veterans of the common war and had demonstrated their value.

Francis Clinton was able to overcome and survive all of the obstacles thrown his way throughout his service in the United States Military. As per my research, he survived everything that life threw at him and overcame hardships that many may give in to or just plain give up.

Let me name a few things he survived: bullets, arrows, persevered and overcame subfreezing temperatures, inadequate equipment, inferior supplies, lack of food and provisions, unsanitary conditions, hatred, violence, hostility, persecution, lynching, discrimination, and racial prejudice. Also, he survived a huge list of deadly diseases like smallpox, chicken pox, tuberculosis, cholera, measles, yellow fever, typhoid fever, typhus, and pneumonia. He endured long, tedious expeditions, hundreds of dangerous missions, being despised, ridiculed, and rejected by many of the officers and the settlers he protected. Even after all of this, he received little to no recognition for his services and duty to his country and for settling the great American Frontier.

In my opinion, Francis should be officially recognized for all his military services.

If you know your history

Then you would know where you are coming from

Then you wouldn't have to ask me

Who the heck do I think I am?

- **Bob Marley**

Francis Clinton Story

Timeline

1842 – Francis Clinton was born – Baltimore, Maryland

1865-67 – Enlisted with Naval Services in 1865 at New Bern, North Carolina

1867 – Fort Leavenworth - Enlisted on May 21, 1867 with 10th Cavalry - Troop E - United States Army as a Private original member when organized (Buffalo Soldier), Ft. Leavenworth, KS

1867-68 – Fort Riley later named Fort Gibson - Company E, 10th Cavalry was assign with Captain George Robinson and Lt. J. Tellonison and detached to Indian Territory

1868 – Fort Arbuckle - Company E, 10th Cavalry operated out of Fort Arbuckle - Helped build Fort Arbuckle

1869-71 - Camp Wichita later named Fort Sill – 10th Cavalry, Company E - instrumental in building the road between Camp Wichita and Fort Arbuckle, also helped construct Fort Sill

1872 – Fort Sill - May 21, 1872 Honorably Discharged at Fort Sill

1873 – 1875 - Fort Sill - Fort Griffin – Camp Supply - Fort Richardson -Re-enlisted with the same organization on February 3, 1873 – Company E, 10th Cavalry transferred to Fort Richardson April and May 1873. Reported he was sick with his right side ruptured. He was injured in the line of duty on the Washita River (Red River)

1875 – Fort Richardson - Fort Concho – April 1875 Regimental Headquarters transferred to Fort Concho

1876 – Fort Concho – Scouting expeditions and detachments

1877 – Fort Concho (Based on the army returns – Feb. – Mar. Apr.) Francis spent a lot of his time scouting and, in the field

1878 – Fort Concho – San Felipe Post- Re-enlisted in the same organization, February 4, 1878 and is on the muster roll for Nov. and Dec. (Based on the army returns – Jan. – Feb.) San Felipe and Ft Gibson

1879 – Fort Concho – Fort Clark - (Based on the army returns) Francis spent a lot of time scouting, patrolling in the field on detachment service and chasing Victorio – Jan.-Mar. June July Aug.

1880 – Fort Concho – Fort Stockton – Fort Davis - (Based on army returns) Oct.-Nov. Detached Service Ft Davis & Ft Concho - He spent a lot of time on detached service (Chasing Victorio) --- (Based on army returns) June 26 Detached Service/Patrol, July – Aug - Admitted to the Post Hospital at Fort Concho, Texas – Nov. 18, 1880 with Frosted Feet contracted in the line of duty. (Dec. 31, 1880 remain under treatment in hospital for frost bitten toes on left foot)

1881 – Fort Concho – Fort Sill - (Based on army returns) January 31, 1881 Remain under treatment for frost bitten toes in Post Hospital - February 28, 1881 returned to duty – June, July, Aug. Detachment Service, In the Field, Escort Duty. (Oct. Sick Nov. Hospital and back to field duty)

1882 – Fort Concho – Return to in the field detach services base on army returns (April, May17, 1882, June-July)

1883 –Fort Concho - February 2, 1883 was honorably discharged from service at Fort Concho, Texas

1895 –Oklahoma Land Run – Homestead (November 5, 1895) Staked out land near Langston, Oklahoma

1897 – Francis married Charlotte Tipkins Clinton

1898 – Clara Clinton Sprencer was born (Gramma Clara Sprencer)

1900 – Cora Clinton was born

1902 – Samuel Clinton was born

1904 – Cleorafell (Cleo) Clinton was born

1906 – Blanch Clinton was born

1909 – Emmitt Tarejoy was born

1912 – Verna Clinton was born

1917 – Death of Francis Clinton

1937 – Death of his dear wife, Charlotte Clinton

Company E, 10th Cavalry
Officers
Captain George T. Robinson
Commanding First Lieutenant John T. Morrison

Francis Clinton 10th Cavalry Troop E was selected to serve in the US Army:

The 84 original enlisted cavalrymen in Troop E organized on June 15, 1867, under Captain G.T. Robinson and Lieutenant J.T. Morrison. Troop E was one of eight Troops organized at the onset.

Enlisted Cavalrymen

1. Henry Adams
2. John Albert
3. Francis M. Blaston
4. Charles Burnham
5. George W. Brookings
6. Francis M. Brown
7. George W. Brown
8. Nathaniel Butler
9. John Carpenter
10. Lewis Carter
11. Richard Clark
12. John W. Clarke
13. Francis Clinton ***
14. Adam Cork
15. Calvin Craddock
16. David Dixon
17. Washington Dumas
18. John Fittiswater
19. Henry Fisher
20. Jefferson Ford
21. George Garnett
22. Franklin Gibbs

23. John Gibbs	43. Charles Key
24. George Green	44. Randall King
25. William Greene	45. Lewis Laoos
26. Robert Hacket	46. Lewis Lyons
27. William Hale	47. Charles Livingston
28. Thomas Hamilton	48. James Lighter
29. Henry Harris (1)	49. Aron Lucas
30. Henry Harris (2)	50. John Lyons
31. Henry Hawkins	51. George Maxwell
32. William Hollier	52. William Mathews
33. James Huley	53. Lewis Miller
34. William Jackson	54. James Miles
35. Frank Johnson	55. William Miles
36. Henry W. Johnson	56. Franis Minor
37. James E. Johnson	57. Henry Moore
38. John Jones	58. Samuel Marti
39. Alfred Jones	59. John W. Nevitt
40. Henry Jones	60. John Parker
41. William H. Jones	61. Frank Perkins
42. Benjamin Kewconda	62. William P. Pierce

63. Nelson Piper

64. William Poper

65. Tony Ratcliff

66. Edward Ross

67. William H. Simmons

68. Augustus Smith

69. James Speaks

70. John Tedder

71. Hardin Thomas

72. Isaac Thompson

73. James Walker

74. John H. Washington

75. Toney White

76. Peter Wilkeson

77. John Williams

78. Norman Williams

79. Ted Wilson

80. Thomas Waley

81. John Thompson

82. James Young

83. John Brown

84. Henry W. Smith

MOTTO: READY and FORWARD

The Buffalo Soldier Emblem:

The Regimental Song of the Buffalo Soldier Tenth Cavalary Regiment
Sung to the tune of Stephen Foster's "Camp town Races."
We're fighting bulls of the Buffaloes, Git a goin' – git a-goin.'

From Kansas' plains, we'll hunt our foes;

A trottin' down the line.

Our range spreads west to Santa Fe, Git a goin' – git a-goin'.

From Dakota down the Mexican way;

A trottin' down the line.

Goin' to drill all-day

Goin' to drill all night,

We got our money on the buffaloes,

Somebody bet on the fight.

Pack up your saddle and make it light.

Git a rollin' – git a rollin'.

You are training fast for a hard fight;

A rollin' down the line.

Untie your horse and boot and gun, Git a goin' – git a-goin'. Shake out your feet, or you'll

miss the fun,

A rollin' down the line.

Goin' to drill all-day

Goin' to drill all night,

We got our money on the buffaloes,

Somebody bet on the fight.

It's Troops in line for the Buffaloes,

Git a movin' – git a-movin'. Then Squadron mass when the bugle blows.'

A movin' into line.

Pull in your reins and sit your horse, Git a movin' – git a-movin'.

If you can't ride, you'll be a corpse;

A movin' into line.

Goin' to drill all-day

Goin' to drill all night,

We got our money on the buffaloes,

Somebody bet on the fight

Fiddlers' Green

Halfway down the trail to Heal

In a shady meadow

Are Souls of all dead Troopers camped?

Near a good old-time canteen.

And this eternal resting place

Is known as Fiddlers' Green

Marching past, straight through to Heal

The Infantry are seen.

Accompanied by the Engineers,

Artillery and Marines,

For none but the shades of Cavalrymen

Dismount at Fiddlers' Green.

Though some go curving down the trail

To seek a warmer scene.

No Trooper ever gets to Heal

Ere he's emptied his canteen

And so rides back to drink again

With friends at Fiddler's Green.

And so when man and horse go down

Beneath a saber keen,

Or in a roaring charge of fierce melee

You stop a bullet clean,

And the hostiles come to get your scalp,

Just empty your canteen,

And put your thinking cap on your head

And go to Fiddlers' Green.

-Unknown

About the Author

Archietta Burch James was born and raised in Oklahoma. She attended Langston Elementary school and Guthrie High school. She received her bachelor's degree in Elementary Education at Langston University, Langston, Oklahoma. She received her master's degree in Elementary Education at Prairie View A&M University, Prairie View, Texas and a second master's degree in Mid-management and Administration at Southwest Texas State University (Texas State University) San Marcos, Texas. She taught various grade levels for almost five decades across the country and is currently enjoying her retirement.

She is launching her writing debut with a book on the life of her esteemed great grandfather, one of the original famous Buffalo Soldiers. Her book is titled "Francis Clinton A Buffalo Soldier, and American Hero."

After listening to stories about him passed down from generation to generation, she was obsessed with researching and writing the true story about his life.

Her hobbies are reading, writing, cooking, walking, meditating, and traveling. When she is not doing those things, she can be found spending time with her loving family that includes her husband Clarence James, Jr., son John James, daughter Iman James, granddaughter Jaylah James, daughter-in-law Leanna James and a host of other relatives.

She currently lives in Garland, Texas.